CONTROLLING RESTAURANT & FOOD SERVICE LABOR COSTS

By Sharon Fullen

The Food Service Professional's Guide To:
Controlling Restaurant & Food Service Labor
Costs: 365 Secrets Revealed

Atlantic Publishing Group, Inc. Copyright © 2003
1210 SW 23rd Place
Ocala, Florida 34474
800-541-1336 .
352-622-5836 - Fax

www.atlantic-pub.com - Web site
sales@atlantic-pub.com - E-mail

SAN Number :268-1250

International Standard Book Number: 0-910627-17-7

Library of Congress Cataloging-in-Publication Data

Fullen, Sharon L.
Controlling restaurant & food service labor costs : 365
secrets revealed / by Sharon Fullen.
p. cm. -- (Food service professionals guide to)
Includes bibliographical references and index.
ISBN 0-910627-17-7 (pbk. : alk. paper)
1. Food service--Labor productivity. 2. Food service--Cost
control. I. Title: Controlling restaurant and food service labor
costs. II. Title. III. Series.
TX911.3.L27 F85 2003
647.95'068'1--dc21
2002013541

Printed in Canada

Book layout and design by Meg Buchner of Megadesign
www.mega-designs.com • e-mail: megadesn@mhtc.net

CONTENTS

6 SCHEDULING YOUR STAFF

7. PRODUCTIVITY

8. PRODUCTIVE BUILDINGS

9. FINANCIAL DECISIONS

INTRODUCTION

From the parking attendant to the chef, the people who serve your customers are your restaurant. You can have a prime location, a beautiful dining room and impeccably prepared food and have it all spoiled by a rude server, sloppy busperson or an inattentive janitor. Your restaurant's success is based upon your ability to locate, hire and solidify a group of people into your Customer Service Team.

The food service industry has long been plagued with an inadequate workforce and exceptionally high turnover rates. The increased demand for service workers and culture changes within the workforce means less-educated recruits, more non-English-speaking employees and fewer younger people interested in restaurant work.

Whether you own a celebrity-filled, trendsetting establishment or a truck-stop diner, the situation is the same. Where do you find good employees? How do you keep good employees? How can you get your money's worth?

Labor costs typically run 25–35 percent of your budget and, depending upon your menu offerings, can equal or exceed your food costs. Keeping your prime costs (food and payroll) in the 60–69-percent range is your profit-making goal. Simply cutting staff won't do it though. Your aim should be to get the highest productivity possible for your money. But to save money without losing quality of service, you have to start at square one.

This guide has been written to help you tackle the never-ending process of reducing your labor costs. You'll find practical ideas and suggestions with immediate and long-term results. We'll be helping you to examine your attitudes and relationships with the people who represent your business; to develop hiring and training programs to "build" great employees and minimize turnover; to create physical and emotional environments that encourage outstanding performances and produce happy employees and customers; and to maximize resources and enhance your profitability.

CHAPTER ONE

FOUNDATION OF SUCCESS

G ood food and good service are the foundation of a successful restaurant. As a service industry, restaurant profit margins are notoriously slim. Your restaurant's profitability is a direct result of your ability to control your "service" costs without sacrificing your customers' needs and expectations.

Service is Paramount

K eep firmly in mind that service is paramount. Surveys show that 83 percent of customers would not return to a restaurant if they experienced "poor service." Sixty-one percent mentioned "slow service" as a factor. However, we aren't just talking about the front-of-the-house staff – every employee plays a vital role in good customer service. If your customer finds better service elsewhere, what do you lose? Just one customer, right? But that customer spent $10 in your establishment twice a week: $10 x 2 = $20 x 52 weeks = $1,040 a year! What if you lose five customers or even ten? One server with a bad attitude can cost you their salary or more in lost revenue and permanently damage your reputation within the community. Good service is a combination of:

- **Strong commitment by management.** Standards and expectations backed by a respect and partnership attitude.

- **Positive employee attitudes and motivation.** A desire and willingness to serve others and good communications.

- **Good training methods**. Top-notch employee skills and abilities.

- **Practical approaches and procedures**. To work together efficiently.

- **Labor-saving devices**. An environment filled with tools and equipment that promote good ergonomics and maximum productivity.

People are Assets

You probably wouldn't think too highly of someone who bought a beautiful automobile and then never bothered to clean it, change the oil or tune it. Who would spend so much and not protect their investment? Well, employing one person can cost as much as a car and, unless you are diligent, you too could be wasting your money!

- **Invest wisely.** Every dollar you spend (directly and indirectly) to "purchase" and maintain an employee is an investment in your business. Protecting your human assets and securing your investment is integral to your labor-saving efforts. Are you investing wisely?

- **High turnover rates.** They leave after three months! Why should I spend the money only to have them move to a competitor? Because the industry creates high turnover rates and you have a responsibility to your business to provide a solution. Exceptionally high food service turnover rates are deeply rooted in historical attitudes and a business model based upon spending as little as possible for workers and your "factory." By ignoring workers' physical and emotional needs, restaurant owners have created an industry filled with some of the "worst jobs."

- **Address problems.** Certainly you cannot solve these

industry problems single-handedly; however, you can play an active role and reap the benefits of addressing such factors as low pay, excessive stress, inferior work conditions, limited career potential, poor economic security and overwhelming physical demands.

- **Costs.** "I cannot afford to pay more!" But you already are. You're paying for it through costly recruiting and training, reduced productivity, increased food costs, inconsistent customer service and larger overhead. By redirecting these dollars towards maintaining and enhancing your human assets, you'll be investing in your business instead of just paying to keep the doors open.

- **Employee satisfaction.** Employee satisfaction isn't just a touchy-feely goal – it's a key to your success. To learn more about building happy and productive employees, read:
  - *Keeping Your Employees* at www.keepemployees.com
  - *First, Break All the Rules: What the World's Greatest Managers Do Differently* by Marcus Buckingham and Curt Coffman
  - *Follow this Path: How the World's Greatest Organizations Drive Growth by Unleashing Human Potential* by Curt Coffman and Gabriel Gonzalez-Molina

Reducing Your People Costs

Notice we said PEOPLE costs. Why? Because if you only think about cutting man-hours, you'll lose site of your objective – to please your customers and be rewarded with profits! Your business success is based upon your success at gathering together a group of workers with different skills and experiences to produce a quality product. Your most valuable asset, your employees, are filled with personal desires and expectations. You must tap into their need to be valued and respected. Here are three outstanding resources on people management, mentoring and building partnerships with your employees:

- *Mind Your Own Business – People, Performance, Profits* by Jim Sullivan. This restaurateur-written book offers excellent advice on hiring and leading employees. For more personnel and customer service advice, visit www.atlantic-pub.com.

- *Managers as Mentors* by Chip R. Bell, a nationally recognized customer service guru. This book explains creating strong employee relations. Also on the Web at www.chipbell.com.

- **Restaurantowner.com** – This site provides extensive guidance for restaurant owners. A "Food for Thought" passage sums up their "people business" philosophy. *"Your effectiveness as an owner or manager is directly related to your understanding of people and the quality of your interactions with your staff."*

Profits are Everyone's Business

As a restaurant owner you have a strong personal motive to be profitable – and so do your employees! Reducing your labor costs wisely and compassionately balances the needs of the organization with the needs of its team members. Reducing your labor costs requires:

- **Good hiring practices.** Search for the right person to fill the job. Look beyond the basic skills for a person that fits your restaurant's personality.

- **Balanced staffing levels.** Schedule ample people to get the job done and satisfy customers without wasting resources.

- **Greater employee productivity.** Teach them how to work smarter, not harder.

- **Excellent people skills.** Communicate well with

managers, line supervisors, support staff and customers. Loyal employees create loyal customers.

- **Sound financial decision-making.** Analyze and invest in labor-savers; research and utilize tax breaks and business support programs.

Management Commitment

Your commitment to quality service is reflected in how you and your management staff conduct themselves. Take a look at your behaviors and actions. Are they how you'd want your employees to act? Below are some though-provoking questions on leadership. A "yes" answer to any of these means you should invoke the first rule of good leadership – leading by example.

- **Do you come to work grouchy?** Your employees will copy your mood. Greet your employees with a happy, friendly attitude; the way you want them to greet your customers.

- **Are you sloppy or careless in your work habits?** Are you late for appointments or forget to follow-up on their requests?

- **Is your appearance unprofessional?** If you dress sloppily, your employees will resent having to meet higher standards and will slowly begin to ignore your dress code.

- **Do you disobey your own established standards?** Pour doubles for your friends at the bar and your bartenders will start to do the same for their friends. If you ladle on extra portions, look for rising food costs because your kitchen staff will stop measuring too.

- **Do you avoid addressing problems when they arise?** When you see someone skirting established standards, promptly and tactfully remind them (but never in front of customers). If you let mistakes slide, soon your standards will be nothing but "hot air."

- **Do you ramble or lecture when answering questions or giving directions?** Keep it short and simple or your employees will "zone out" and miss the point. Always make sure they understand.

- **Do you feel they should do whatever you ask because you're the boss?** Mutual respect plays an enormous role in good leadership. Respect is something you earn and not just because you sign the paychecks.

- **Do you share your goals with your employees?** Help reduce employee discontent by sharing your short- and long-term business goals. They'll feel more valued and in greater control of their work.

- **Formal written policies and procedures are very important for setting standards.** However, a large part of setting standards is done through leading by example.

CHAPTER TWO

BUILDING YOUR TEAM

Hiring Team Members

Hiring is the start of a long-term relationship between employer and employee. Or at least it should be. Can you imagine hiring a full staff of qualified workers and having them stay with you for years? This is rare in the restaurant business, but it isn't an unattainable goal. Hiring is more than just finding warm bodies to fill positions. You need to find competent, hard-working people who are a good fit for your restaurant personality. Hiring the "best" applicant, even if they don't meet your standards, will cost you in the long run.

Your Challenge

Your challenge as a restaurateur is to balance your business needs with the needs of the people who will spend the majority of their day in the service of your customers. Perhaps your greatest challenges as an employer are the economic realities of a service industry where the majority of jobs are low paying with low social status. Federal reports show food prep and serving wages average $7.72 an hour and 75 percent make less than $8.50 an hour – the lowest wages among the major occupational groups studied. The result is a shortage of service workers and turnover rates of 250 percent for line staff and 100 percent for managers.

Restaurant Employee Classifications

Your mix of employees will include seasonal, part-time, full-time and career-oriented employees. The list below is in pyramid order - with the top level being the smallest number within an organization and by highest to lowest salary.

- **Executive careers.** Comprehensive fiscal responsibility, college educated, may report to owner and/or stockholders (President or CFO).

- **Managerial careers.** Manages people and/or things, college educated (General Manager or Human Resources Director).

- **Artisans.** Creative talent, may be self-taught based on natural abilities, on-the-job training or career training (Lead Chef or Pastry Chef).

- **Skilled workers.** Valuable skills acquired from work experience or schooling (Bookkeeper, Wine Steward).

- **Semi-skilled workers.** More complex task with indirect supervision, some prior experience or training (Server or Baker).

- **Unskilled laborers.** Manual tasks with direct supervision, no special training (Janitor or Busperson).

The Right Person for the Job

Finding the right person for the job starts with a solid understanding of what your business team needs. As the saying goes "You can't get what you want, if you don't know what it is."

Before you start recruiting, you need to make some decisions that will become the basis for a written job description. The following sections will help you gather your thoughts and prepare for the writing process.

Clarifying Your Needs

Whether you are hiring your first employee or adding to a staff of 75, there are five primary areas you should consider before you place that classified ad.

1. Tasks employee(s) must accomplish.

2. Skills and experience employees must possess.

3. Training levels you are willing to or must provide.

4. Personality and attitude your customers expect.

5. Budget available for salary, taxes and benefits.

Tasks

Identify the tasks (duties) that must be completed during the shift, week, month and beyond. Categorize each activity by:

- **What they will do?** Detail action (e.g., clean, cut and store salad ingredients; accept food delivery, compare to packing list, sort and store; or answer phone, accept and schedule reservations).

- **Where they will do it?** Front- or back-of-the-house.

- **When they will do it?** Before, during or after active serving times.

- **How often they must do it?** Daily, weekly, monthly or other.

- **What is a success?** What is acceptable performance? What is award-winning performance?

Skills and Responsibilities

Classify each task by skills required and level of responsibility. Typically, the greater the skills and responsibility level required, the higher the salary you'll pay. Identify areas where less-costly labor can be used or whether you should reward someone for accepting more responsibility.

- **Skill level.** Management skills: dining room supervisor, beverage manager. Prep skills: pastry chef, sauce cook. Customer service skills: server, bartender. Support staff skills: busperson, receiving clerk.

- **Responsibility level.** P & L responsibility: executive chef, banquet manager. Reports "as needed" to superior: soup cook, baker. Empowered to act on behalf of restaurant: receptionist, dining room manager. Direct daily supervision: server, bartender. No significant decision-making duties: dishwasher, janitor.

Skill and Experience Training Expectations

All good companies train constantly. Learning is a never-ending process that enhances employee skills and your service quality.

- **Consider comprehensive training.** Comprehensive job training programs and perhaps even life skill training may be needed. New hires with little to no prior work experience or no food service history can be developed into loyal employees through in-house mentoring and training or work-study programs.

- **Trainee jobs.** Some restaurant positions are, by nature, trainee jobs. In this case, your job description will also include an outline of the training program that the new hire must complete before moving beyond their probationary period.

- **Developing skilled workers.** With restaurant owners nationwide routinely reporting a shortage of skilled workers, you may be forced to develop your own experienced workers. This means many positions may have to be filled by trainees.

Your Budget

Employee wages are influenced in each community by the cost of living, available workforce, competition and social status of the position. Your financial ability to pay for certain skills and training may limit your expectations for a position. Your compensation package (salary and benefits) must be appropriate for the duties and responsibility outlined in the job description.

Whether you've written several pages of job tasks or just scribbled some thoughts on a napkin, it's time to start writing an overview of the job you seek to fill.

Writing Job Descriptions

A job description is a detailed definition of a job and a list of the specific tasks and duties the employee is responsible for daily, weekly and monthly. The more complete the job description, the simpler the task of training. A good job description will help you and your staff to:

- **Hire the best candidate** for the job.

- **Understand required job skills** and expected responsibility levels.

- **Develop and complete training programs.**

- **Create goals for employee growth** and potential salary increases.

Job Description Tips and Resources

Below are some ideas and resources to help you create useful job descriptions.

- **Ask your staff.** Their input can be invaluable. You'll also discover opportunities to redistribute duties and reward better employees with "prized" assignments.

- **Incorporate attitude standards.** Descriptions should include attitude standards like, "Will answer phone with cheerful voice within five rings."

- **Hire a human resources expert.** Find expert help from the Human Resources Consultants Association (www.hrca.com) and the Society for Human Resources Management (www.shrm.org).

- **Have an attorney or human resources consultant review for legality.** Well-written job descriptions can help you defend yourself in wrongful termination or other employee litigation. However, they can also work against you.

- **Review job descriptions posted on the Web.** Use keywords "restaurant job description" and "[insert job title] job description" to see how other restaurant owners explain the position.

- **Buy a book.** Contact the National Restaurant Association at 800-482-9122 and request publication MG999, Model Position Descriptions for the Restaurant Industry.

- **Buy a pre-written job description.** Jump-start the process by purchasing job descriptions from sites like HR Net at www.atlantic-pub.com. American Express offers a handy interactive tool at the Small Business Resource site home3.americanexpress.com/smallbusiness/tool/hiring/intro.asp.

- **Read about creating job descriptions.** Business Owner Tool Kit at www.toolkit.cch.com/text/ P05_0300.asp; or National Restaurant Association articles at www.restaurant.org/business/ bb/2000_05.cfm; and www.restaurant.org/rusa/ magArticle.cfm?ArticleID=754

.

Your Employee Package

Employees are "paid" in a variety of ways: wages, tips, meals, profit sharing, bonuses, commissions, insurance coverage, vacations, tuition reimbursement, childcare assistance, transportation subsidies, retirement plans and family leaves.

Paying minimum wage and offering no benefits is one way to keep your labor costs low. But rarely will you be hiring the best available and you'll constantly be dealing with high turnover and employee dissatisfaction. Although money isn't the only motivator, it certainly is an important factor in attracting and retaining quality employees. You've got to think creatively and act aggressively to design a cost-effective, yet "valuable" employee package.

Wages

No other industry has such divergent wage standards between federal, state and local jurisdictions. The Fair Labor Standards Act (FLSA) established federal work standards. However, these do not apply if state or local laws are more stringent.

- **Federal law.** Federal law requires that you pay the minimum wage ($5.15 per hour - 2002) for all hourly employees (except those who receive more than $30 a month in tips) and youth wages ($4.25 per hour – 2002) for the first 90 days. Superceding laws may require that the prevailing minimum wage be paid even if the worker earns tips; others allow for a reduced hourly rate for tip earners. To learn more about wage regulations:

- **Visit the Department of Labor site** at www.dol.gov for current wage and hour laws and links to state information or contact your local State Employment Division.

- **State minimum wage rates** at www.dol.gov/esa/ minwage/america.htm.

- **Tipped employee wages by state** at www.dol.gov/esa/ programs/whd/state/tipped.htm.

- **National Restaurant Association.** Read what the National Restaurant Association has to say about minimum wages at www.restaurant.org/legal/ law_minwage.cfm.

Gratuities

In recent years, IRS and court rulings have created a lot of headaches for the restaurant industry in regards to taxing tips. With ongoing litigation, your best bet is to read the current legal bulletins produced by state and national restaurant associations. The National Restaurant Association provides tip resources for employers and employees at www.restaurant.org/legal/tips/resources.cfm. To protect your business from IRS audits and tax liabilities:

- **Encourage your employees to accurately report tips.**

- **Hold employees responsible for tip income** by having them read and sign a form that explains tipping rules.

Employee Benefits

Fringe benefits are an important part of compensating your employees. These are all voluntary rewards and enticements, as the law does not mandate them. Don't overlook the emotional impact (self-esteem, peace of mind, confidence, security and safety) these have on employees when developing your package.

- **Web sites.** To learn more about employee benefits, visit BenefitNews at www.benefitnews.com, BenefitsNext at www.benefitsnext.com or CCH Business Owner's Tool Kit at www.toolkit.cch.com.

- **Provide time-off benefits.** Include a leave policy in your personnel manual. See www.toolkit.cch.com/ tools/persleav.rtf for a sample policy.

- **Holidays.** Pay for closed holidays or offer comp time for open holidays.

- **Sick days.** Grant a set number of annual sick days. But to encourage attendance, offer a cash bonus for unused days. Allow staff to convert sick days to family leave or vacation days.

- **Vacations.** How employees take their vacation can create some unnecessary payroll costs. Learn about potential savings at www.toolkit.cch.com/ text/P05_4385.asp.

- **Family leave.** Help reduce employee stress by offering family leave options. You might offer short leave periods for bereavement and funerals and extended leaves for maternity/paternity/adoption or long-term family care. For information on family leave under the Family Leave and Medical Act (FLMA), see the Department of Labor information at www.dol.gov/elaws/fmla.htm.

- **Other time off.** Jury duty, voting and military leave may be required by law in your state.

- **Offer discounted meals for employees dining with immediate family members.** Thank workers and their families, who may dine out infrequently.

Costly (But Valuable) Benefits

Employers who provide the "costliest" benefits are providing employee peace of mind and security. Although these benefits can escalate your total payroll costs, their value can be significant. Many of these benefits simply would be financially unattainable without even limited employer support.

- **Invest in health insurance coverage.** Unless it's financially prohibitive, health insurance coverage should be your most touted benefit. Employer-paid premiums are rare; but sharing the cost and exploring partially self-insured plans can make this more affordable for everyone. This is the most desired benefit for job applicants.

- **Talk to your accountant and financial advisor about retirement plans.** Stock options, 401(k) plans and IRAs can be created to attract career-minded individuals. Visit www.dol.gov/pwba/ compliance_assistance.html for information on federal pension plan laws under the Employee Retirement Income Security Act of 1974 (ERISA).

- **Offer life and long-term care insurance.** Employees can benefit from tax-free life insurance coverage (up to $50,000) and long-term care insurance.

Where to Find Your Next Employees

Many owners will tell you the hardest part of operating a restaurant is finding enough good employees. Searching for new employees can become almost a full-time job. Don't wait until you have a vacancy to develop contacts and personnel resources from which to draw from at a moment's notice. Building your team members requires a continual proactive search effort. Overall, it's most cost-effective for a business to hire a fully qualified and experienced employee. So how do you find one? Below we've outlined a variety of places and ways to find loyal, hard-working employees.

- **Employee referrals.** Personal referrals can be strong candidates, as your reliable employees will typically have good friends. Offer a referral bonus of $50 to $300 (perhaps even more for managerial hires).

- **Your competitors and peers.** When you encounter an experienced worker when dining out, discreetly give them your card and let them know you are hiring and thought he or she might be a good candidate.

- **Your customers.** Another reliable referral. Long-term customers have a good feel for your environment and are great "word-of-mouth" advertising.

- **Headhunters.** Top managerial and "talent" positions may require a headhunter. These employment specialists typically have connections and contacts within specific industries. Expect to pay up to 33 percent of the new hire's first year salary.

- **Employment agencies.** Semi-skilled workers can be found through employment agencies but fees typically can outweigh benefits.

- **Trade organizations.** State and national hospitality and food service organizations offer employment services.

- **Employment open house.** Creating an open and friendly atmosphere puts potential employees at ease, builds great word of mouth and establishes your business as a desirable workplace.

- **Job fairs.** Set up a booth at community job fairs. Sell your restaurant as a great place to work with great people.

- **Unions.** Many restaurateurs are "fearful" of unions, but quality employers who offer competitive compensation packages and good working conditions shouldn't hesitate to take advantage of their job banks.

Advertising for People

Help wanted advertising is a common method for locating unskilled and semi-skilled food service employees. However, classified ads won't typically attract sufficient candidates for skilled, artisan and managerial positions. The key is to select a medium (print or Web) and publication where your potential employees will be looking.

- **Classified ads.** Place text or display ads in print and electronic publications. Local newspapers, school papers and ethnic (native language) newspapers for your entry-level/trainee, unskilled and semi-skilled positions. (See The People You'll Need for definitions of these job classifications.)

- **Your Web site.** Include a link on your restaurant Web site to a "We're Hiring" page detailing job opportunities and application procedures.

- **Trade associations.** Post jobs and search resumés at state and national restaurant associations' and hospitality associations' online job banks, newsletters and magazines. Many hospitality and food service organizations also offer personalized recruitment services and training support.

- **The National Restaurant Association** offers links to industry-specific employment sites such as www.restaurant.org/careers/jobs.cfm, as well as job search information at www.restaurant.org/careers/ employers.cfm, and food service publications at www.restaurant.org/business/resources_ magazines.cfm.

- **Job site listings.** For skilled and executive staff, tap into the workforce around the world at general sites: Monster.com at www.monster.com, FlipDog at www.flipdog.com, America's Job Bank (national and state) at www.ajb.dni.us, EmploymentGuide at www.employmentguide.com, CareerBuilder at www.careerbuilder.com and LatPro (for Spanish- and Portuguese-speaking managers and professionals) at www.latpro.com.

- **Industry-specific job sites.** Search Web directories and search engines by such keywords as "restaurant jobs," "food service career" and "chef" for employee/employer matching sites.

- **Summer job sites.** Connect with students and recent graduates seeking summer work: A+ Summer Jobs at www.aplus-summerjobs.com, Seasonal Employment at www.seasonalemployment.com/summer.html and Summer Jobs at www.summerjobs.com.

Tips for Writing Powerful Ads

Want to write the ad yourself? Consider these resources:

- **Use ad-writing software** from Power Hiring at www.powerhiring.com/coach/features/AdWizard.asp.

- **Learn ad-writing techniques** from JobsOnline at www.jobsonline.com/how_to_write_job_ad.asp; TotalJobs.com at recruiter.totaljobs.com/forrecruiters/ knowyourstuff/getstarted/index.asp; or SCORE www.score.org/workshops/want_ad.html.

- **Hire an expert writer at** AdWriter 123 at www.adwriter123.com; Dr. Nunley at www.drnunley. com/drnad.htm; or search the Web for "freelance copywriter."

More Places to Find Help

- **State employment divisions.** Every state maintains a job bank of potential workers. Some states work like a private employment agency (but with no costs to you) to actively match employees and employers.

- **Cable TV.** Cable advertising can be surprisingly inexpensive. Your initial ad development cost can be amortized over several ad campaigns. Your local cable company can assist with ad production.

- **At the movies.** On-screen advertising can be a great way to connect with potential employees as most moviegoers are in your targeted age group.

- **Billboards.** Although not inexpensive, billboards can potentially reach thousands every day with your "help wanted" message.

- **Radio.** Ask your best employees for their favorite radio stations to reach potential team members. Radio stations can handle everything in-house for you.

- **Resumé "archives" and rehires.** High turnover rates means workers are frequently shopping for another job. "Leftover" or rejected applicants may be the right match now! Former employees (providing they left in good standing) may have found "the grass isn't greener" elsewhere and be interested in returning.

- **Senior centers.** Need mature part-time support? Many active seniors are seeking to reenter the workforce.

- **Foreign worker agencies.** Some service industries have discovered the benefits of hiring experienced foreign workers. More details on hiring foreign workers can be found at the U.S. Department of Justice at www.ins.usdoj.gov/graphics/services/tempbenefits/ TempWorker.htm and the Department of Labor at www.workforcesecurity.doleta.gov/foreign/hiring.asp.

- **Human resource sites** such as www.safehr.com/ hiring_foreign_nationals_and_imm.htm and www.workforce.com/section/03/article/ 23/26/49.html offer information on foreign-worker programs.

Trainees for Hire

What do you do if you cannot find the right person for the job? Create one! Here are some ways to locate and develop people with potential:

- **High school and community college career centers.** Develop relationships with career counselors who can direct potential part- and full-time employees to you.

- **Trade (food service, hospitality and restaurant management) schools.** Work with guidance counselors to find students needing financial assistance. Participate in work-study programs.

- **Students.** Start your outreach before the student graduates. Offer tuition reimbursement or full sponsorship in exchange for guaranteed employment.

- **U.S. Armed Services.** Thousands of well-disciplined and dependable people leave active duty every year seeking civilian employment. See Corporate Gray Online at www.corporategrayonline.com, Transition Assistance Online at www.taonline.com and Department of Defense at www.dmdc.osd.mil/ot/linkpage.htm.

- **Federal, state and local full-employment programs.** Government, non-profit and faith-based programs offer employees a helping-hand. Employers' benefit from financial subsidies (reimbursement and tax credits), counseling and off-site training.

- **Displacement, relocation, internship and school-to-work programs.** Reach out to laid-off workers, rural areas (with typically higher unemployment) and high school and college students seeking a direct career path.

- **Special-need labor pool.** Reentry programs for the disabled, single mothers, welfare recipients, retirees, high-risk youth, Veterans and non-English speakers.

- **Foreign-born (non-English speaking) job placement services.** English as a Second Language (ESL) training for workers and cultural advice for employers.

- **Ticket to Work and Work Incentive Improvement Act** (employing the disabled). Department of Labor at www.dol.gov/odep/pubs/ek00/ticket.htm.

- **Social Security Administration** at www.ssa.gov/work/Employers/employers.html.

- **Veteran employment.** Department of Labor at www.dol.gov/vets.

- **Welfare-to-Work** at www.mnwfc.org/wotc/empacket.pdf.

- **Overlooked labor pools.** Thousands every year needing a second chance and "life saving" can be loyal and dependable workers, if given a chance. Like the "special-need" work pool, there are numerous programs that provide financial, educational and transition support for employers and employees. Contact such groups as:
  - **United Way of America** at www.unitedway.org
  - **Job Corp** at www.jobcorps.org
  - **Poor People's Guide** at www.poorpeoplesguide.org/ guide/employment.html

Outsourcing, Temps & Leasing

Have an occasional need for a specialist? Need extra hands for a banquet or large event? Don't want to waste your time on personnel matters?

- **Seek out consultants** to provide you with decorating, floral arranging, bookkeeping, marketing and other "as needed" activities. Check your local Yellow Pages, Business-to-Business Directory, Better Business Bureau membership roles or restaurant association.

- **Explore independent contractors.** These freelancers are responsible for all of their employment taxes, workers' compensation insurance, etc. Be aware of the regulations on using independent contracts by visiting Nolo Law For All at www.nolo.com/lawcenter/index.cfm or speaking with a legal advisor.

- **Use a temporary services agency** that specializes in food service personnel. You pay a set fee and they handle everything from screening to payroll taxes.

- **Borrow an employee.** In developing good relationships with other restaurant owners, you should explore referrals for workers who are looking to moonlight or pick up a few hours of extra work.

- **Lease an employee.** No hassles here as the leasing firm handles all human resources activities. This isn't typically a cost-effective option, but circumstances may warrant it. Beware of "hiring" clauses that penalize you for direct hiring of placed individuals. For more information on employee leasing firms, also know as a Professional Employer Organization (PEO), visit PEO.com at www.peo.com/peo; National Association of Professional Employer Organizations at www.napeo.org, 703-836-0466; Institute for the Accreditation of Professional Employer Organizations at www.podi.com/iapeo, 301-656-1476; and National Association of Temporary and Staffing Services at www.natss.org, 703-549-6287. Get a free payroll analysis and National Restaurant Association membership discounts by contacting PEO Brokerage, Inc. at www.saveonpayroll.com/dineout, 877-592-4389.

A Diverse Workforce

When hiring and keeping food service employees turns into a full-time job, nurturing and growing dependable employees from diverse backgrounds becomes a necessity. Creating a diverse workforce is good for society and it's good for business. Below are some helpful suggestions and resources on creating a strong and diverse staff that includes the disabled, elderly, minorities, gays, women and people from various cultures and ethnic backgrounds.

- **Buy a book such as:**
  - *Workplace Diversity/A Manager's Guide to Solving Problems and Turning Diversity into a Competitive Advantage: A Manager's Guide to Solving Problems* by Katharine Esty.

  - *The Diversity Toolkit: How You Can Build and Benefit from a Diverse Workforce* by William Sonnenschein.

  - *Peacock in the Land of Penguins* by B. J. Gallagher Hateley, Warren H. Schmidt.

- **Take a class on diversity.** Contact local universities and community colleges for management to learn how to smoothly transform a group of individuals into a cohesive team. For online classes at World Learning, see www.worldlearning.org/solutions/index.html. Research videos on diversity from Newsreel at www.newsreel.org/ topics/diversity.htm.

- **Take time to learn about other cultures.** Sometimes language isn't the only barrier. Cultural differences may cause miscommunication, hard feelings and work problems. Working with people from specific cultures and ethnic groups requires patience and a willingness to learn.

- **Search the Web** and read articles using keywords like "diverse workforce," "diversity" and "equal opportunity." Look for articles like *Supervising Across Language Barriers* at agecon.uwyo.edu/RiskMgt/humanrisk/ SupervisingAcrossLanguageBarriers.pdf; and *Hiring and Managing a Culturally Diverse Workforce* at agecon.uwyo.edu/RiskMgt/humanrisk/Hiring&Managin gaCulturallyDiv.pdf.

- **Explore local minority-support organizations** for English as a Second Language (ESL) classes, diversity programs and educational support.

- **Work with non-profit organizations** to develop equal opportunity and diversity programs. Good places to start are Goodwill Industries at www.goodwill.org, National Business & Disability Council at www.business-disability.com, National Adult Literacy at www.nala.ie, American Association for Affirmative Action at www.affirmativeaction.org, and National Organization for Women at www.now.org/ issues/wfw/index.html.

Employee Search Resources

Dozens of national employment and food service industry sites can be excellent places to search or advertise for future employees. Below you'll find industry-specific sites to start your outreach.

American Culinary Federation
www.acfchefs.org

Bartending Jobs
www.bartendingjobs.net

Careers in Food
www.careersinfood.com

Chef 2 Chef
www.chef2chef.net/pro/jobs

Chef Jobs
www.chefjobs.com

Chef Jobs Network
www.chefjobsnetwork.com

ChefJob.com
www.chefjob.com

Chefs at Work
www.chefsatwork.com

Chefs Employment
www.chefsemployment.com

Culinary Job Finder
www.culinaryjobfinder.com

Culi-Service Jobs
www.culiservicesjobs.com

Entrée Job Bank
www.entreejobbank.com

Escoffier
www.escoffier.com/classifieds.html

Fine Dining Jobs
www.finediningjobs.com

Food Industry Jobs
www.foodindustryjobs.com

Food Work
www.foodwork.com

FoodService.com
www.restaurantjobs.org

Hospitality Career Net
www.hospitalitycareernet.com

Hospitality Careers Online
www.hcareers.com

Hospitality Classifieds
www.hospitalityclassifieds.com

Hospitality Jobs
www.hjo.net

Hospitality Link
www.hospitalitylink.com

Hospitality Online
www.hospitalityonline.com

Hotel and Caterer Jobs
www.hotelandcaterer.com

HotelRestaurantJobs.com
www.hotelrestaurantjobs.com

I Hire Hospitality Services
www.ihirehospitalityservices.com

Just Restaurant Jobs
www.justrestaurantjobs.com

Management Search Associates, Restaurant Division
www.best-restaurant-jobs.com

My Food Jobs
www.myfoodjobs.net

Nation Job Network
www.nationjob.com/restaurant

National Restaurant Association
www.restaurant.org/careers/jobs.cfm

Need Wait Staff
www.needwaitstaff.com

On The Rail
www.ontherail.com

Pastry Whiz
www.pastrywiz.com/talk/job_toc.htm

Resources in Food
www.rifood.com

Restaurant Careers
www.restaurantcareers.com

Restaurant Jobs
www.restaurantjobs.com

Restaurant Jobs
www.rjobs.com

Restaurant Jobs Store
www.restaurantjobstore.com

Restaurant Manager
www.restaurantmanager.net

Restaurant Staffing
www.restaurantstaffing.com

RestaurantBeast.com
www.restaurantbeast.com

RestaurantManagers.com
www.restaurantmanagers.com

Sommelier jobs
www.sommelierjobs.com

WineWingsWaitStaff.com
www.winewingswaitstaff.com

Selecting the Right Candidate

If you've done a good job in attracting qualified candidates, you should have a stack of resumés and applications. Unlike other fields, well-qualified workers may struggle with the written word and multiple jobs are typical. Below are some tips on how to select the best candidates for face-to-face interviews.

- **Read between the lines.** Does this person have the right experience? Spot-check references if there are red flags.

- **Why are they leaving their current position?** Applications should ask the reason for leaving. When checking references, verify why the employee left. Conflicting stories isn't a reason to toss the application, but it is a red flag needing attention.

- **Is the application neat and legible and filled out properly?** If they can't fill out an application properly, how well will they do with writing guest checks, ringing up sales or following recipe directions?

- **Are they a short-timer?** If they change jobs every few months, they will most likely do the same with you. If everything else looks good, you may want to interview them anyway, but keep it in mind and explore why they move around so much.

- **Conduct phone screenings.** You can learn a lot from a 2-minute phone call. Always ask questions that require more than yes or no answers.
  - What are your career goals?
  - What income level do you expect?
  - What kind of career growth would you like?
  - Ask one to three questions that verify a person's knowledge and skills.
  - Ask about work history gaps.

- **Listen carefully and use your instincts.** Is the person articulate and friendly? Are they hard to reach? Be careful what you ask. Many traditional interview questions are no longer legal or wise.

Getting Ready to Interview

Your next step is to schedule face-to-face interviews.

- **Choose from three to six candidates.**

- **Set interview dates at least 2 days in advance** for local applicants and 2 weeks in advance for out-of-state applicants.

- **Explain when, where and how long the interview will be,** format of the interview and what (if anything) they should bring with them.

- **Tell them if you'll be conducting tests.**

- **Provide adequate directions** along with a contact name and phone number.

- **Set aside ample time for each interview** and a half-hour break between. The break will give you time to rest (interviewing can be an intensive process) and to jot down notes and reminders.

- **Be prepared.** Put together handouts and company introduction materials to present your restaurant as a great place to work. Create a quick tour to show off your facility and introduce candidates to key employees.

- **Improve your interview skills.** There are plenty of good books, classes, videos and Web sites to help. If you are nervous or inexperienced at conducting interviews, practice. Role-playing can be a great way to improve your interview skills. Rent tapes on learning how to improve interviewing skills and techniques from Web sites like www.interviewing-skills.com/gutfeeling.html. Job Interview (www.job-interview.net/index.htm) is a great site for interview advice, or read one of these books:
  - *High-Impact Hiring: How to Interview and Select Outstanding Employees* by Del J. Still (2001).

  - *Hiring the Best: A Manager's Guide to Effective Interviewing* by Martin Yate (1993).

  - *96 Great Interview Questions to Ask Before You Hire* by Paul Falcone.

The Interview Process

The interview process can be stressful and nerve-racking for everyone! Your job as an interviewer is to elicit information from an uncomfortable interviewee while being a mind reader, psychologist and salesperson. You'll be asking probing questions, listening intently, judging attitudes and appearances and trusting your managerial instincts. Below are some helpful resources for interviewing and selecting qualified employees.

- **Web resources.** For restaurant-specific advice, visit consultant Simma Lieberman Associations at www.simmalieberman.com/articles/interviewemp.html. For recruiting and selecting hourly employees, see Hire Tough at www.hiretough.com. For hiring systems, visit Unicru at www.unicru.com. For interviewer training, see Hanigan Consulting at www.haniganconsulting.com/training/index.htm.

- **Understand what characteristics, skills and experiences you need** and what you can live without. Refresh yourself by reading through the job description and preparatory notes.

- **Record your notes immediately.** Remember, just like the employee, you're under stress and your memory can falter. Also, don't take any notes that might appear to be discriminatory. These are all fair game for opposing attorneys!

- **Be prepared to answer the tough questions.** You should be able to answer salary, benefit and advancement questions along with work expectations and your business stability.

- **Never over-promise.** Don't indicate there are advancement opportunities when none exist.

- **Give them your full attention.** Emergencies happen, but as opposed to conducting an interview on the run or while you are distracted, reschedule it.

- **Create an interview team.** Include supervisors and team leaders in the interview process. They can help you select people who not only have the skills but also the attitude your restaurant needs.

Asking Probing Questions

Be careful what you ask. Some questions are against the law; while others should be avoided to protect you and your business from discriminatory claims. For a list of illegal interview questions, visit Office.com at www.office.com/syb_illegalquestions.htm.

- **Ask all your questions at once.** This puts the burden on the interviewee instead of on you. It will also keep you from talking too much or leading the interviewee to the answers you want to hear.

- **Ask essay-style questions that can't be answered with yes or no.** Use your own style of speaking, but ask questions such as:
  - What would your former employer or coworkers have to say about you?
  - Who was your best boss and why?
  - Describe your favorite job.
  - Was there anything at your last job that you didn't get a chance to do or learn?
  - Describe a disagreement you had with a supervisor and how you resolved it?
  - If I were your boss, what would be the most important thing I could do to help you be successful?

- **Work at making interviewees feel comfortable.** Some back-of-the-house staffers may be too nervous to ask questions. Beware of servers or front-line people that have a problem speaking up.

- **Bring the interview to a close with, "We have about five more minutes."** When people know they're running low on of time, they get down to what is really important to them. Often this last-minute exchange can cement your impression of the candidate – sometimes positively and sometimes negatively.

Listening Intently

- **Watch the interviewee.** Do they fidget and constantly change position? If you're hiring for a high-energy position, this might be the right person. If what you are looking for is a calm, controlled employee, they might not be the best choice.

- **Improve your listening skills** with help from the International Listening Association at www.listen.org.

- **Learn to interpret body language.** Read about the signs in "Interview Body Language: It's Not What You Said" at MBA Jungle, www.mbajungle.com. Also, learn how cultural differences can cause you to misinterpret body language at equalopportunity.monster.com/ articles/ignorance.

Judging Attitudes and Appearances

- **Did they show up on time?** Someone who is late for an interview has a good chance of being late for work. Of course, if they have a flat tire, be reasonable. How they handle being late is equally important.

- **How are they dressed?** You wouldn't expect a prospective server to show up in a suit, unless you have a very high-class establishment. But a sloppy, slovenly interviewee will surely be a sloppy, slovenly employee. Are fingernails clean, hair washed and clothes neat?

- **Do they look around and show interest during your tour?** If they have no interest in what may be their future place of employment, how much interest will they have if you hire them?

- **Does the interviewee respond in a friendly manner when introduced to other employees?** A friendly attitude and outgoing personality is vital for good customer service.

Pre-Employment Reviews

Screening and assessment tests and checks are frequently used during the pre-employment stage to unearth high risk, unqualified or dishonest candidates. Many companies believe that investing in pre-employment screening helps to reduce turnover, protect your business and select qualified candidates. Here are an assortment of resources and articles to help you decide whether your restaurant could benefit from pre-employment procedures:

- **Skill and aptitude tests.** See Hire Success at www.hiresuccess.com/aptitude.htm; Employee Selection & Development, Inc. at www.employeeselect.com/basicAptitude.htm; Psychological Services, Inc. at www.psionline.com; or Reid London House at www.reidlondonhouse.com.

- **Assessment products and services.** See HRtest.com at www.hrtest.com; Saterfiel at www.saterfiel.com; or Evaluations at www.evaluationslc.com.

- **Restaurant manager test** from Pan Testing at www.pantesting.com/products/ResourceAssociates/ rma.asp.

- **Personality tests.** See Personality Tests for Business Management at www.personality-tests-personality-profiles.com; 123 Personality Tests at www.123-personality-tests.com; or Guidelines for Selecting Personality Tests from FurstPerson at www.furstperson.com/pdf/PersonalityTestGuide.pdf.

- **Background checks**. See U.S. Search.com, Inc. at www.ussearch.com; or Privacy Rights Clearinghouse (Fact Sheet #16) at www.privacyrights.org. Why conduct a background check? The reasons are explained at AbsoluteBackgrounds.com at www.absoluteback-grounds.com/employers-why.htx.

- **Drug screening.** See Employment Drug Testing at www.employmentdrugtesting.com; or National Drug Screen at www.nationaldrugscreen.com.

- **Testing software.** See a food service test software package at www.hrpress-software.com/food.html.

Hiring the Best Person for the Job

Unfortunately, there is no exact science for making your final choice. However, you can improve your chances for success with good hiring practices. We've gathered some informative sources for tools and guidance to help you choose your next employee.

- **Research.** Read two excellent articles on selecting the right employee:
    - Lyons Associates Executive Search – *Choosing the Right Candidate* at www.club-jobs.net/right_candidate.htm.

    - My Web (The Site for Small Business Owners) - *Choosing Between Two Equally Qualified Candidates* at www.mywebca.com/infolibrary/staffing/staffing7.htm.

- **Conduct multiple interviews if necessary.** First impressions can be deceiving and second (or even third) interviews can reveal new facts. Use the second interview to bring in other interviewers and to discuss wages and benefits.

- **Check references thoroughly.** Failing to check references can be a costly mistake. You could be hiring a poor worker or someone with excessive absences. You could be risking a negligent hiring lawsuit where an employer can be held liable when they knew, or should have known, that an employee presented a foreseeable risk of harming others. Monster.com offers excellent advice to employers on reference checking at hr.monster.com/archives/hiringprocess/reference. Employment Marketplace talks about your right to check references at www.eminfo.com/articlesection/ ReferenceChecking.htm. Career Know-How, www.career-knowhow.com/resumes/fibs.htm, reports these job-seeker statistics:
  - 51 percent falsify length of past employment and salary.
  - 45 percent falsify criminal records (remember, you can only ask about convictions, not arrests).
  - 33 percent lie about driving records.

- **Non-work related references.** Entry-level workers, with little or no prior work experience, should provide teachers, pastors, scoutmasters or other responsible adults as references.

- **Hire a reference-checking company.** Companies like HRPlus, www.hrplus.com; Employment Screening Services, www.employscreen.com; and Info Link Screening, www.infolinkscreening.com can get the full scoop and save you hours of phone calls.

- **Don't tell all the candidates of your decision until your new employee starts.** You may find that the chosen candidate changes his or her mind at the last moment. This way your second choice doesn't feel like one!

CHAPTER THREE

SAVING PAYROLL DOLLARS

Saving Payroll Dollars

Savvy entrepreneurs never overlook allowable tax deductions, credits, government programs, business subsidies or other money-saving opportunities. Some will be easy to take advantage of, while others will require some diligence and extensive paperwork. However, the direct and indirect savings can go a long way to balancing your budget. Below you'll find some valuable resources and ideas on trimming payroll costs. The information provided here is for your educational benefit. Please consult with your accountant, tax advisor or attorney for current information and applicability to your situation.

- **Pay employees with benefits.** The more cash wages you can move into exempt and pre-tax categories, the less payroll taxes you and your employees will pay!

- **Benefits fall into three categories: taxable, exempt and pre-tax.** Taxable benefits are subject to federal income tax withholding, Social Security, Medicare or federal unemployment tax. They are reported on Form W-2. Exempt benefits are excluded from employee withholdings and employer contributions (some exceptions) and are not reported. Pre-tax benefits feature flexible benefit plans that allow employees to design and pay for customized benefit packages with nontaxable employer dollars. They can cover accident and health costs, adoptions, dependent care and life insurance.

- **Create charts and employee guides to demonstrate how employers can "earn" more by saving tax**

dollars. Use these tools during the hiring process and employee orientations to help employees to understand the advantages of receiving benefits over a larger paycheck.

- **Properly calculate overtime pay for tipped workers.** To verify whether you are accurately calculating overtime rates, review the information available from the National Restaurant Association at www.restaurant.org/legal/law_ot.cfm#meals.

- **Review your workers' compensation premiums.** Studies show many businesses routinely overpay for workers' compensation. A very informative article can be found at www.bizjournals.com/denver/stories/2000/11/13/focus3.html. Search for assistance at sites like Cut Comp, www.cutcomp.com; and Workers' Comp Info, www.workerscompinfo.com.

- **Keep track of time.** Good recordkeeping can trim payroll costs up to 7 percent. Check out manual, electronic and computer-based time clocks with thumbprint ID sign-in at Konetix, www.konetix.com; and Time Clock Plus, www.timeclockplus.com.

Offer the Right Benefit Package

Employee compensation packages are comprised of taxable wages (employee and employer paid) and taxable (employee) and non-taxable benefits.

- **Implement pre-tax benefit plans that save everyone money.** A variety of benefits can be packaged where deductions would be pre-tax (prior to withholding calculations). Retirement, commuting, dependent care and medical savings plans can all be paid with pre-tax dollars, such as section 125 Plans ("cafeteria" or "flex" plans).

- **Explore benefits that cost almost nothing, but save you payroll dollars.** Although many employers contribute to benefit plans, you can set up 100-percent employee-paid plans where your only costs would to administer the plan and file IRS Form 5500. See Benefits Essentials at www.benefitsessentials.com/Lite/BELibrary/Cafeteria.cfm; BenFlex, Inc. at www.beneflexinc.com; My Cafeteria Plan at www.mycafeteriaplan.com; U.S. Health Plans at www.ushealthplans.com/medsavings.shtml; or learn more about 401(k) plans at www.401khelpcenter.com.

- **Hire a benefit consultant.** Companies like Broad Reach Benefits, Inc., www.brb1144.com/index.html, can guide you through establishing voluntary benefit programs and expand your benefit choices.

- **Offer tax-exempt employee benefits.** Explore with your tax advisor the benefits of offering these fringes (wage deduction figures given are per employee/per year):
    - Achievement awards – personal property award up to $1,600 tax free.
    - Adoption assistance – $10,000.
    - Athletic facilities – value to employees.
    - Dependent care assistance – up to $5,000.
    - Education assistance – up to $5,250.
    - Employee discounts – formula based on cost.
    - Group-term life insurance – contact IRS for current regulations.
    - Meals – up to 100 percent of costs. Read about de minimus (little value) meals and workplace meals at www.5500accountant.com/meals-and-lodging.htm and in IRS Publication 15-B.

Tax Deductions & Credits

We've outlined some potential wage and tip tax-saving ideas that you should discuss with your business advisors:

- **Let an expert guide you!** Your first step to savings should be to hire a qualified CPA. Many payroll-related activities require strict compliance with court rulings, IRS opinions and state and federal laws that change frequently.

- **Keep current on tip tax laws and court rulings.** The restaurant industry continues to tackle the issue of tips and their tax obligations. Recent rulings have been in the IRS's favor but the discussion continues. Your local restaurant association can keep you and your accountant up to date. For current information and tip reporting guides, visit the National Restaurant Association's tip reporting page at www.restaurant.org/legal/tips; call the IRS at 800 TAX-FORM; or download www.irs.gov/pub/irspdf/p1872.pdf.

- **Protect yourself from an audit by agreeing to a standard tip calculation method.** The IRS agrees not to audit your tip records if you agree and comply with either the Tip Rate Determination Agreement (TRDA) or the Tip Reporting Alternative Commitment (TRAC). For more information, visit the Restaurant Report at www.restaurantreport.com/departments/ac_tiptactics.html.

- **Take a 45(B) credit.** The IRS allows businesses to take a credit against Social Security and Medicare (FICA) taxes paid on tips. To learn more, read the National Restaurant Association's article at www.restaurant.org/legal/law_fica.cfm.

- **Claim wage credits and deductions for employees' meals.** Meals provided in your restaurant for your convenience are not taxable. If your staff must remain on site during their shift, meals provided are not taxable as wages. Meals used as rewards or outside of the employees' scheduled work period are typically taxable. Meals provided at no charge may be credited against your employer's minimum wage obligation. Some states set specific values for meal credits while the Fair Labor Standards Act (FLSA) allows the "reasonable" cost as an offset.

- **Claim wage credits and pay exemptions for extended breaks.** Typically, rest periods longer than 30 minutes and where no work duties are required, are not compensable. Check the following Department of Labor links for information on your state's rules: For state laws on rest periods, see www.dol.gov/esa/ programs/whd/state/rest.htm. For state laws on meal periods, see www.dol.gov/esa/programs/ whd/state/meal.htm.

Take Advantage of Benefit Discounts and Subsidies

- **Join trade, business or community organizations** to lower benefit costs. Many offer reduced pricing on insurance, wellness programs, incentive plans, training and retirement packages. Contact your state's restaurant association and the National Restaurant Association at www.restaurant.org/join/services.cfm to learn more about industry offerings. Small business organizations can provide reduced rates for members. Try one of these to reduce your employee benefit costs: National Business Association at www.nationalbusiness.org or Small Business Benefit Association at www.sbba.com.

- **Offer discounts for lifestyle and health needs** like prescriptions, vision, dental and cosmetic surgery. EhancedBenefits.com, www.ehancedbenefits.com, offers such plans for as little as $16.50 per month.

- **Seek out discounts and subsidies for free or low-cost employee benefits** such as bus, subway or train passes. CommuterCheck.com has an excellent article illustrating your potential tax savings at www.commutercheck.com/Tax_cut.html.

- **Create a carpool and ride-share program.**

49

Employers' subsidies promote the reduction of urban traffic and energy usage. Information is available through federal, state and local government energy and transportation departments.

- **Barter with local merchants** for pizza, movie passes, theater tickets and other items suitable for employee rewards. Consult your tax advisor regarding your tax obligation and record-keeping requirement.

- **Contact your bank for employee-banking services** including free checking, discounted loan services and automatic payroll deposit.

- **Enroll your business with a credit union.** Credit unions offer employees excellent discounted financial services. Convenient on-site enrollments are available.

- **Set up a U.S. Savings Bond program.** Funds are deducted from each paycheck, held until the purchase price is accumulated and then the employee's bond is ordered. For information, visit www.savingsbonds.gov.

- **Explore employee discounts on auto and home insurance.** An example can be found at Broad Reach benefits at www.brb1144.com/auto_home.htm.

- **Offer no-cost life skills classes.** Seek out bankers and investment counselors to provide free financial advise on savings, borrowing, investing, retiring and owning a home. Nonprofit and government organizations can be good sources for free classes on topics like parenting, choosing a child care provider and health concerns.

Government Employment Programs

Government agencies frequently take active roles to help high-risk and disadvantaged people become employed by offering payroll subsidies, tax breaks and training programs. There are also financial-support programs based upon where your business is located and the type of benefits you offer.

- **Search out work programs,** subsidies and tax breaks by contacting your local chamber of commerce, small business associations and State Departments of Welfare, Commerce and Employment and your accountant. A good example of a state tax incentives program is Florida's Workforce detailed at www.onestopahead.com/tax_incentives.htm. Also, ask about your state employment division about "empowerment or enterprise zone" tax credits.

- **Read IRS Publication 954** "Tax Incentives for Empowerment Zones and Other Distressed Communities" to learn about federal wage (salary plus company paid health insurance costs) credits.
  - Distressed communities (up to $3,000 per employee).
  - Native American employment credits (up to 20 percent credit).
  - Work opportunity credit for high unemployment groups, e.g., felons, veterans, food stamp recipients, (up to $2,400 per employee/$1,200 summer youth employee).
  - Welfare-to-Work (up to $8,500 per employee).

- **Help the disadvantaged and your business.** Training programs and tax credits and deductions are available. Disadvantaged – CCH Inc. (www.cch.com) has an informative article on the four federal tax credits listed above at taxguide.completetax.com/text/Q16_3214.asp. Contact Disadvantaged - U.S. Work Force at www.usworkforce.org, 877-US2-JOBS.

- **Disadvantaged adult training.** Information on training programs, apprenticeships and more is available at the Department of Labor, www.doleta.gov/programs/adtrain.asp.

Disabled Worker Programs

The federal government defines "disability" as a physical or mental impairment that substantially limits one or more of the major life activities, for example, walking, seeing, speaking or hearing. Under the Americans with Disabilities Act (ADA), employers are to make "reasonable accommodation" to facilities, job duties, work schedule, equipment and other accommodations. A "qualified individual with a disability" means an individual with a disability who, with or without reasonable accommodation, can perform the essential functions of the employment position that such individual holds or desires.

- *Restaurant and Institutions Magazine* (see article at www.rimag.com/022/Opsb.htm) speaks of the 50 million disabled Americans as "overlooked resources" for the food service industry.

- **Learn more about the financial benefits of hiring the disabled** under the Ticket to Work and Work Incentive Improvement Act (TWWIIA) at the Department of Labor, www.dol.gov/odep/pubs/ek00/ticket.htm.

- **Improve your accommodations for disabled workers** and accessibility for disabled employees and/or customers. The Disabled Access Credit (IRS Code Section 44) grants small businesses a tax credit (a 50-percent credit up to $5,000 annually). Details are available from the Department of Labor at www.dol.gov/odep/pubs/ek97/tax.htm. Expenses covered are:
  - Sign language interpreters for employees or customers with hearing impairments.
  - Readers for employees or customers who have visual impairments.
  - Purchase of adaptive equipment or the modification of equipment.

- **The Architectural/Transportation Tax Deduction**

(IRS Code Section 190), www.dol.gov/odep/pubs/ ek97/tax.htm grants small businesses up to $15,000 a year for expenses incurred in removing barriers for persons with disabilities. Amounts above the $15,000 maximum annual deduction can be depreciated. Expenses covered are:

- Accessible parking spaces, ramps and curb cuts.
- Telephones, water fountains and restrooms accessible by wheelchair.
- Walkways at least 48-inches wide.

- **Businesses may take both the Section 44 credit and the Section 190 deduction** in the same year providing the activities qualify.

Other Helpful Tax-Savers

- **Share credit card fee costs.** Before disbursing tips added to credit card charges, you may legitimately deduct the credit card company's processing fee on the tip portion. Be certain to verify if this is allowed in your state.

- **Hire family members to eliminate some tax obligations.** Many restaurants are unincorporated family businesses where everyone capable of working does. If your children or spouse aren't on the payroll and they can legitimately handle some type of work, you may be eligible for a variety of tax breaks. For example, hire your under-18 child and don't pay Social Security or federal unemployment taxes. Speak with your tax consultant for specifics. Read the Motley Fool article at www.fool.com/taxes/2002/taxes020628.htm.

- **Explore other tax deductions and credits related to benefits.** Many are tax-free to employees and all are legitimate business deductions. Below are a few tax savers:
  - Up to 50 percent of employee pension plan set-up costs.

- Up to $100 a month per employee for public transportation discounts or passes.
- Up to $180 per month per employee for parking.
- Clothing (uniforms, aprons, hats) imprinted with the name of your business can be considered an advertising expense.

Hidden Payroll Expense Savings

You'll also have other costs associated with payroll. It takes time and money to maintain time slips, calculate taxes, write payroll checks, keep payroll records, administer benefit programs and make tax deposits. To help you with the paperwork hassles and reduce these costs, we've compiled some practical ideas and useful resources.

- **Hire a local payroll service firm.** Even if you handle your own bookkeeping, outsourcing payroll can be a wise decision. You won't have to worry about the right tax table or when to deposit withholdings. One advantage of hiring a professional is that they frequently assume all liability for filing errors and pay for all penalties or interest on late or inaccurate filings. Be certain to ask about liability issues.

- **Try online payroll services.** Search the Web under the keyword "payroll service" for banks, national service firms, local consultants and Web-based solutions. Ask about liability issues. See Wells Fargo Bank at www.wellsfargo.com/biz/products/payroll/payroll.jhtml; QuickBooks at www.intuit.com/quickbooks/ products/payroll/index.shtml; Paychex at www.paychex.com; or Automatic Data Processing at www.adp.com.

- **Buy payroll software and do-it-yourself.** Popular accounting packages have add-on modules and stand-alone software programs. Remember, you assume all liability for errors. See QuickBooks at

www.quickbooks.com/services/payroll; Peachtree at
www.peachtree.com/epeachtree/payroll.cfm; Pensoft
(restaurant versions) at www.pensoft.com; or Restaurant
Technology Inc. at www.internetrti.com/ProductTours.

- **Use human resources software, online services and
  downloadable human resources forms.** See Trak It
  Solutions (HR software) at www.trak-it.com/
  welcome.html or HR Next (forms, job descriptions) at
  www.hrnext.com/tools.

- **Find someone to do the human resources support
  and paperwork.** Human resource consultants and
  personnel service providers can handle every aspect
  from advertising to interviewing to overseeing your
  benefit plans.

- **Eliminate writing payroll checks.** Direct deposit
  paychecks into employee bank accounts. Some banks
  even offer free checking for employees needing to open
  a bank account associated with your direct deposit par-
  ticipation.

- **Consider lengthening your payroll periods.** You can
  reduce your payroll accounting costs (check writing,
  record keeping) by up to 70 percent by switching from
  weekly to monthly. If employees find the monthly cycle
  difficult, try offering a less-costly procedure like a
  scheduled draw mid-month. To verify your state's pay
  period requirements, see the Department of Labor's
  chart at www.dol.gov/esa/programs/whd/
  state/payday.htm.

Other Payroll Resources

- **Tax Tip Calculator** at www.paycheckcity.com/TipCalc/
  tipCalculator.asp.

- **Time and attendance software listings** at www.hr-software.net/pages/211.htm.

- **Days off calculator** at www.schedule-me.com/calc.htm.

- **Pay raise calculator** at www.payraisecalculator.com

- **Discounted benefits for National Restaurant Association members** through Palmer & Cay at www.palmercay.com.

CHAPTER FOUR

TRAINING EMPLOYEES

Teaching Success

Accepting the responsibility for training is expensive, so your first choice should be to hire people with experience. Paying more than the prevailing wage and offering a comprehensive benefit package may cost you less in the long run. If you are lucky enough to have an ample well-educated workforce in your community, your employee training may only consist of orienting new hires to your own procedures and establishing personal goals and employer expectations. However, if trained workers aren't readily available, your only option may be to accept the responsibility of bringing their skills up to your standards.

Invest in Training

- **Invest time and money in training** to improve productivity, increase sales and enhance quality.

- **Allocate work time to properly train your employees.** Their increased productivity will pay for your time and investment

- **A good job description = better training = more productivity.**

Reasons for Training

- **Unprepared employees are unhappy employees,** resulting in high turnover.

- **Unskilled or untrained employees will cost you more** in low productivity, poor service, waste and inefficiency.

- **Lack of training creates employees with poor attitudes** and bad work habits.

Train the Trainer

If you didn't hire someone for their training abilities, don't expect them to be a natural at it. Simply handing over a new employee to a coworker may work, but most often it won't. Your first step is to train the trainer.

- **Teach employees to be trainers** with help from Workforce.com at www.workforce.com/section/11/article/23/24/25.html. and www.atlantic-pub.com.

- **Food safety training tips and techniques** from Food Safety Training & Education Alliance at www.fstea.org/resources/training.html and www.atlantic-pub.com.

- **Find a "Train the Trainer" seminar.** Restaurant management-specific classes and seminars are available through your state's restaurant association.

Your Training Needs

You pay for training, whether it is done right or wrong. Protect your investment by developing a program that meets the needs of your organization and brings you the greatest benefits.

- **Look at your current employees.** What natural talents do they have that need to be enhanced? What would they like to learn? Talk to them and review their current skills against their assigned job description.

Which tasks were still as difficult for them as when they started their job? These tasks should move up higher on your training schedule.

- **Start cross-training.** Cross-training is teaching your employees how to do a job (or even specific tasks) other than their own regular job. This can be very valuable, especially to a smaller operation. Cross-trained employees can fill in when others are absent and jobs can be combined during slow economic times. Cross-training can also be used to prevent boredom for employees with routine jobs. Rotating positions can make the work more interesting.

Specific Training Areas

Below are some training areas from which your employees and restaurant might benefit:

- **Computer.** Personal computer hardware, computerized systems such as sound and lighting systems, computerized equipment.

- **Software.** Point-of-sale systems, time management, scheduling, inventory control, reservation system.

- **Language.** English for immigrants or foreign languages to converse with non-English-speaking employees or customers.

- **Safety.** Food and alcohol, personal and workplace safety (accident prevention, injury, ergonomics), theft and robbery.

- **Legal.** Discriminatory practices, sexual harassment.

- **Purchasing.** Inventory control, waste management.

- **Leadership.** Problem solving, motivational.

- **Personnel management.** Problem employees, disciplinary, hiring, firing, sexual harassment, discrimination
  prevention, diversity.

- **Time management.** Productivity improvements
  through time management.

- **Communication skills.** Peer-to-peer, employee-
  employer, customer contact, phone skills, grammar,
  vocabulary.

- **Customer service, sales techniques.** How to increase
  ticket sizes without offending customers, handling
  difficult customers, building customer relationships.

- **Etiquette.** Personal, phone, cultural differences.

Setting Goals and Expectations

New employee orientation is where you'll lay a foundation
for success by establishing your expectations of their
performance and set productivity and performance goals.
These aren't just something you announce and then never
revisit. Goals and expectations are benchmarks for future
employee reviews, bonus systems and salary increases. Here
are some practical suggestions and resources to help you
explain your performance standards and set success goals.

- **Establish your basic employee standards.** See how
  McDonald's addresses basic employee expectations at
  www.mcdonalds.com/countries/usa/careers/expect.

- **Learn more about setting expectations** from Allman
  Consulting at www.allmanconsulting.com/articles/
  clear_expectancy.htm.

- **Read an e-book from Restaurant Trainers** at www.restauranttrainers.com/html/goal_setting.html.

- **Work with employees to discover their career path.** Goal setting is more than just stating someone must cover 7 tables and serve 24 customers an hour or they won't get a raise. It's also working together to develop a career. Many food service careers are based upon on-the-job training and advancing through the ranks. You have a personal opportunity to transform a trainee into a talented chef or valuable manager.

- **Build in rewards and incentives.**

- **Explain how their success relates to the success of their department and your operation.** Employees that understand how they can make a difference accept increased responsibility and think more often about the common good. Personnel motivators call this "owning" the job.

- **Establish schedules and deadlines whenever possible.** It's only human nature to delay actions until the very last minute. By setting deadlines and regular performance reviews, you'll keep the goals active.

- **Provide the tools and resources to reach goals.** This can be something as simple as a book to read or as comprehensive as an educational subsidy.

- **Develop goals together and ask for a commitment.** Give employees a copy of agreed-upon goals and expectations. Place a signed copy in their employee file.

Establishing Quality, Productivity & Performance Standards

For proper training and performance evaluation, you need to have established standards for each job description.

These become your training, proficiency and motivational guidelines.

- **Quality standards.** Quality standards can be difficult to express. You should do your best to illustrate these in words (job descriptions) and demonstrations (on-the-job training). Show servers what the dinner salad should look like (along with appropriate weights, measures and other food-control specifications) rather than telling them!

- **Performance standards.** The information you gather becomes the basis for your training, motivational and employee review efforts. These standards also take into account human factors. Only machines can be expected to consistently perform each task exactly the same way in the same amount of time.

- **Not a weapon.** Work standards shouldn't be used as a weapon or threat – but as a guideline. You cannot reduce a warm smile or a melt-in-your-mouth dessert to a standard.

- **Writing them down.** These standards should all be in writing. Besides including them in operational manuals and job descriptions, create and display wall charts. Use performance improvements between employees or shifts as the basis for a contest or bonus program.

Productivity Standards

The fast-food industry has become exceptionally adept at calculating down to the second how long it takes from the moment the customer walks up until they leave bag in hand. In a single quick-service restaurant, 30 seconds can translate into thousands of dollars annually. To follow are some helpful tips on setting your restaurant's productivity standards.

- **Gather and analyze data.** The better your data, the more accurate your standards will be. Take time and elicit your staff's assistance in setting productivity standards.

- **Conduct studies using actual real-world situations.** You or a productivity consultant should do time and motion studies. This is also an excellent time to review ergonomics and procedures for wasted time and motion.

- **Gather data from other sources.** A wide variety of data may already be available from credit card transaction time stamps, POS and inventory reports, equipment timers and usage calculators, and time clocks. Host/hostesses, servers and cooks can gather information during their days. For example, to calculate steps taken, purchase inexpensive pedometers.

- **Don't rely on "industry standards."** Food prepared and served, facility size, layout and equipment factors are different for every operation.

- **Set realistic minimum activity levels.** This is your benchmark figure. Remember that trainees and experienced staff members cannot be expected to perform at the same level. However, everyone must be able to meet the minimum activity level.

- **Created tiered performance standards.** Start with your minimum standard level and then add an "experienced" level and an "expert" level. These additional levels can be used in incentive programs.

- **Use your most productive employees to set optimal standards.** No employee can or will perform at 100-percent capacity 100 percent of the time. Your goal is to average as high as possible as compared to the optimal productivity standards. Depending on the task and employee experience, acceptable levels will range from 75 percent and up.

- **Express all standards by the amount of work that can be completed within a set time** and the qualitative level of performance required. For example, 25 racks of dishware, flatware and glassware to be washed, dried, sorted and returned to storage area C in two-hour off-peak periods of 8:30 a.m. to 10:30 a.m., 2:30 p.m. to 4:30 p.m. and 11:30 p.m. to 1:30 a.m.

- **Hire an expert.** ProSavvy at www.prosavvy.com or Food Consultants Group at www.foodconsultants.com can help you locate a consultant.

Training Plans

Take your standards and job descriptions and develop a training plan for each job. This will make it clear to a new employee the skills, tasks and behaviors that they must master by the end of their training period.

- **Analyze the job description.** Identify the specific duties to be done and the skills needed to do them. List the duties from the most basic to the most specific.

- **Don't think of it as school.** Your training shouldn't resemble a high school class where everyone would rather be anywhere else! School means memorizing facts and figures, not learning practical skills. Hands-on and face-to-face is the best way to teach because we master skills better by doing.

- **Use hands-on training and practice sessions.** The quickest way for an employee to learn new tasks is through on-the-job demonstrations and immediate practice.

- **Use role-playing for new employees who will be dealing with the public.** You want to make sure they understand their duties and can perform them before you send them out to take care of actual customers. For example, have someone play the part of a customer to test a new server.

- **Test employees on a few critical issues.** Some food-handling and safety facts should be tested to ensure that your employees understand and can comply with regulations. As the cliché goes: ignorance is no excuse but it can be quite costly!

- **Ask them.** "Any questions?" is a simple and powerful way to determine what people need to know. Also try, "Is there anything we haven't addressed?" or "Should we go over that again?" Reward people who speak up and encourage all questions.

Starting Off Right

Even experienced employees need training to start them on a good path. Employee retention starts from day one. Don't just expect them to show up on Monday morning and be ready for work. You must be ready to start them off right.

- **Orientation.** Orientation is your first training session. Don't just hand them a W-4 to complete and a policy manual. Good employer/employee communication starts here!

- **Tell them.** Tell them what you and your company stands for and how important their success is to you and your team. Tell them what you're willing to do to make them a better employee and the benefits of building a future with your company.

- **Make it memorable.** Don't drone on and on. You can even break the orientation into segments to be held over several days.

- **Inject some humor.** Try these tapes and books for ideas: Humor University offers free tips at www.humoru.com/training-topics.htm. *The Big Book of Humorous Training Games: Dozens of Games for Popular Training Topics, from Customer Service to Time Management* by Doni Tamblyn, Sharyn Weiss. Rent or purchase videos from TrainingABC.com, www.trainingabc.com.

- **Avoid technical words or jargon.** New employees are less likely to ask questions, so your point may be lost unless you keep it simple.

- **Demonstrate whenever possible.** Miscommunication can reduce productivity or create unsafe situations.

- **Cover the important topics first.** Think about what you'd want to know and cover those first.
  - How do I get paid? Make certain people understand how to complete and turn in time cards. Explain pay cycles, draws and benefit deductions.
  - To whom do I report? Clearly identify direct and indirect supervisors and explain the relationship.
  - Whom do I ask? Tell new hires about each person's expertise and duties through personal introductions.
  - How do I work it? Allow ample time for equipment training. Lack of training directly impacts employee and equipment productivity.
  - Don't overlook common items such as phone systems and time clocks.
  - Create cheat sheets and reminders for quick reference.
  - Concentrate on ergonomics and safety training.

Meetings

A quick meeting before the shift starts gives you an opportunity to teach and listen. You can also use this time to recognize individual accomplishments and share personal updates; improve communications and reduce gossip; give pep talks and announce contests; and make everyone feel included. Feeling "in on things" is very important to employees.

- **Don't try to solve the world's problems.** But do listen to what your people have to say. You don't have to come up with a solution on the spot.

- **Make problem-solving a team project.** Implement solutions to previously voiced problems during these meetings. When your employees know that you are listening and trying to make their job better, you may be amazed at the solutions they can suggest themselves!

- **Create an atmosphere of trust.** If you ask for input but your people have nothing to say, then you don't have their trust, especially if you overhear mumbled complaints after the meeting is over. To be effective, listen to their complaints and suggestions with an open mind, and to come up with a fair and reasonable solution.

Culinary and Hospitality Programs

Building a relationship with one of the 1,700 culinary and hospitality trade schools nationwide can mean you'll get "first pick" from the most talented students. However, these graduates are still trainees in the sense that they have yet to perform day in and day out! You'll also find high school, community college and university programs to help you develop your own employees. Also contact your state Employment Division for other employee development programs. Below are several resources for locating schools and programs dedicated to the culinary arts.

- **Trade schools.** Search 4 Culinary Schools at www.search4culinary-schools.com; National Restaurant Association at www.restaurant.org/careers/schools.cfm; Star Chefs at www.starchefs.com/helpwanted.html; Culinary Education at www.culinaryed.com; Cooking

Culinary Arts Schools at www.cooking-culinary-arts-schools.com; CookingSchools.com at www.cookingschools.com; and Culinary Training at www.culinary-training.com.

- **Industry programs.** Sponsor a student. A CookingSchools.com article aimed at potential culinary students has some great ideas for potential employers. Go to www.cookingschools.com/articles/scholarships to learn more.

- **Learn about apprenticeship programs** from the American Culinary Federation at www.acfchefs.org or HospitalityCampus.com's online training at www.culinaryconnect.com. You'll find dozens of industry links at www.pexc.com/linkset.html.

In-House Training Programs

Below are resources and tools for enhancing your in-house training programs.

- **Atlantic Publishing,** www.atlantic-pub.com, markets books, videos and training programs.

- *The Waiting Game: The Ultimate Guide to Waiting Tables* by Mike Kirkham.

- *The Restaurant Training Program: An Employee Training Guide for Managers* by Karen Eich Drummond and Karen A. Drummond.

- **Trade Secret training products** from Bill Main at store.yahoo.com/tradesecrets/index.html and online consulting at www.profittools.com.

- **Food safety and skills training from Restaurant Workshop,** www.restaurantworkshop.com.

- **e-Learning and CD-ROM food service courses** from Tap Series, www.tapseries.com.

Adult Education

A dult illiteracy costs U.S. businesses an estimated $225 billion annually in lost productivity. Workplace literacy isn't just an issue for non-English-speaking workers. American born-and-raised adults also lack the training to read written instructions, do basic math calculations or complete a job application properly. Many restaurateurs have discovered the benefit of supporting, sponsoring and offering adult education classes: greater productivity, fewer errors and increased workplace safety. To support employer efforts, a variety of private and public funding, tax benefits and wage subsidies are available.

- **Literacy.** Visit the National Institute for Literacy organization at www.nifl.gov. Watch an interactive presentation on adult literacy in the restaurant industry by the state of North Carolina at www.ncrtec.org/pd/cw/ rest/start.htm. Develop a workplace literacy program. For information, visit the Adult Literacy Organization at www.adultliteracy.org/wpl.html.

- **(GED) The General Educational Development** credential was created as a solution for adults who did not graduate from high school for one reason or another. To learn more about GED testing, visit the Center for Adult Learning at www.acenet.edu/calec/ged.

- **English as a Second Language.** Adult ESL is the term used to describe English instruction for non-native-speaking adults. The goal of ESL instruction is English language (speaking, writing, reading and comprehension) and literacy proficiency. Unlike general adult educational programs, ESL programs may be offered to highly educated learners who simply lack English proficiency. Read "Communicating In a Melting Pot" from Restaurants USA at

69

www.restaurant.org/rusa/magArticle.cfm?
ArticleID=106. Learn more from the National
Association for Bilingual Education (NABE) at
www.nabe.org or call 202-898-1829.

- **Life skills training.** Life skills represent the knowledge
  and aptitudes necessary for a person to function inde-
  pendently and to keep a job. Workers lacking economic
  and educational opportunities may not have developed
  these basic skills and may struggle to meet employer
  expectations. Helping your workers develop life skills
  can be a wise investment. To learn more, Work Shops,
  Inc. has a manual online at www.workshopsinc.com/
  manual/TOC.html.

CHAPTER FIVE

EMPLOYEE SUPERVISION

Leadership

It takes a leader to "create" and maintain productive employees. Do you see employees as diamonds-in-the-rough, ready to be polished? Or are they just warm bodies that meet an immediate need for a short period of time?

- **Being a good boss.** The two commonly sited reasons why employees leave are: they feel unappreciated or they hate their boss. These don't have to be employee issues in your business. Being a good boss doesn't come naturally to some people, but the good news is that you can learn how by reading books, taking classes and watching training videos.

- **Improve your leadership skills by reading.** *The Gifted Boss: How to Find, Create and Keep Great Employees* by Dale A. Dauten. *How to Become a Great Boss: The Rules for Getting and Keeping the Best Employees* by Jeffrey J. Fox. Discover what employees say makes a good boss at Business Research Lab's Web site, www.busreslab.com/bosses/goodboss.htm.

- **Selecting other good leaders.** As your business grows, you'll be increasing your management staff. In doing so, you should be looking for good leaders. A good leader is a good teacher.

Lead by Example

Leadership begins with your own actions and attitude. Below are some simple actions you can take to show your commitment to your goals. Your number-one goal should be good customer service. Second should be productivity. Here are a few simple ways to impress this standard on your employees:

- **Walk through the dining room regularly.** If a customer needs something, get it for them. You will impress the customer that they have been taken care of by the owner, and if your server is too busy to get it, they will remember your willingness to help. If the server was slacking off, and you have hired good people, they will double their efforts so that you don't have to do it again.

- **Jump in and help if food is coming from the kitchen slowly**. If this is a common problem, find out what is causing the slowdown and fix it.

- **Supervise your host/hostess.** Make sure they are aware of the workload on each server and seat people accordingly. Not by number of people, necessarily, but by the difficulty of serving each group. A rowdy group or a group with small children would be more difficult to take care of then the same number of casual adults.

- **Give your help a challenge.** See if you can clear a table before they get to it. Again, if you have hired correctly, they will do everything in their power to clean those tables before you get to them.

- **Replace people who just can't meet acceptable performance standards.** Train them properly and give them encouragement. Counsel them if they fall short. But if they can't make the grade, you have to let them go. The counseling shows your fairness, but removing an employee who isn't doing their job shows your commitment to your business and to your other employees. Good employees shouldn't have to cover the workload for employees who can't make the grade.

Empowering People

One of the most powerful tools you have is to empower your people. Employees that act like owners are more profit-motivated and more productive. Create a team by empowering employees to work for the common good. Create a profit-based incentive program and teach them how inattentiveness and waste costs everyone.

- **Learn how to create a team.** Here are some excellent articles and books on team building, empowering and delegating. *Empowering through Open Communication* by James Harris Group, www.jamesharrisgroup.com/Article-Empowering.htm. *Customers as Partners (Building Relationships that Last)* by Chip R. Bell. *Knock Your Socks Off Service Recovery* by Ron Zemke and Chip R. Bell. *Motivating at Work: Empowering Employees to Give their Best* (a Fifty-Minute Book) by Twyla Dell and Michael G. Crisp.

- **Help your staff understand what it costs to run a restaurant.** Show them your invoices for utilities, rent, insurance, food and beverages. If they understand just how "expensive" it is to do business, they'll be better prepared to make cost decisions.

- **Review time-saving procedures and ideas** with your management and service staff to determine whether they make economic sense for your restaurant. Remember that the best way to get these changes to pay off is to get everyone to buy into them.

Employee Motivation

Employee motivation is an ongoing process that starts at the first interview. As a leader, you are responsible for discovering what motivates your employees. As a businessperson, you are responsible for increasing productivity and spending your resources wisely.

- **Motivating your employees** means you are: developing a partnership attitude; creating camaraderie and team spirit; improving attitudes and resulting behaviors; stimulating and challenging employees to grow; rewarding positive behaviors; mentoring and enhancing lives; and building dedication and loyalty. Keep Employees (www.keepemployees.com) is an excellent site detailing motivational factors.

- **What motivates people.** In a national survey, hundreds of employers were asked, "What motivates your employees?" The majority answered "More money." But when their employees were queried, money ranks in the middle. Employees listed their morale boosters as: interesting work; appreciation and recognition; feeling "in on things"; job security; and good wages. Notice that all of these are subjective. Remember, it's how they feel about a situation (as opposed to the facts) that counts. So how do you figure that out? You ask them!

Interesting Work

Admittedly, some restaurant duties aren't very interesting. So what are you to do?

- **Stimulate them with training.** There's always plenty to do in a restaurant, so why not cross-train the dishwasher to get her out of the kitchen or encourage employees to learn completely new skills. Don't let people limit themselves. Remember, the most renowned chefs in the world started at the bottom!

- **Give them more responsibility.** Expand their duties and delegate more!

Employee Attitudes

Some employers take on the role of Ringmaster when dealing with employees. They wear the uniform and weld the whip as if they were orchestrating a three-ring circus. As lion tamers soon learn: motivating with a whip is short-lived and they are often growled at! Nor do you have to be the head clown to keep people happy. There are times where you'll be wearing your Ringmaster hat and other times when the big clown feet are more appropriate.

- **As Ringmaster, your job is to** oversee an employee's attitude (good or bad) and be aware of how it affects the organization. Determine whether it's a training or attitude problem. Guide people to better attitudes. Reprimand or terminate someone for a "bad" attitude when it becomes a "bad" behavior.

- **Evaluate employees on an informal basis regularly.** Your staff needs to hear what they are doing well and how to improve their weak areas. A major source of stress is not feeling in control. Use this process to help them feel in control of their work lives.

- **Watch for a change in attitude.** A change (for the worse) in attitude is your signal to pay attention now. Attitude problems can quickly decrease productivity and invite theft or sabotage.

- **Listen carefully and don't ignore the signs.** Your mother may have taught you to ignore gossip, but in this case it can give you a heads-up. A poor attitude is a red flag signaling a problem. Take time to isolate the source of employee frustration.

- **Figure out the basis for productivity issues.** Some attitude problems are really training issues. A wise manager once said, "If she could do it when you put a gun to her head, it's an attitude problem. If she can't, it's a training issue."

- **Act decisively.** As the cliché goes – it only takes one bad apple to spoil the barrel. Poor attitudes can "spoil" an organization, so don't hesitate to control the situation with a reprimand or termination.

Challenge Your Employees

Highly productive and service-conscious employees are made, not born. They are a product of their work environment. Hire the right attitude, train properly, reward outstanding performance and guide them in the right direction to build a successful team.

- **Expect the most from people.** People will often surprise you (and themselves) by rising to the occasion when expectations and standards are set high!

- **Make change a priority.** Making at least one change every month shows your employees that you are actively working to make your business better. Even small changes can accomplish this end. And if your employees are expecting and used to changes, they will accept bigger changes more readily.

- **Have a "no stupid questions rule."** Encourage employees to ask plenty of questions. You'd be surprised at how often a "stupid" question is the one everyone is afraid to ask. These are also signals that your training in insufficient.

- **Reward thinking.** Encourage and reward creative problem-solving and cost-saving solutions.

- **Be able to explain why.** As any small child knows – "because" isn't an answer. You must be able to explain the reasons for procedures to your employees. If they don't know why things are to be done a certain way, they will take shortcuts. In some cases this can improve productivity, so be open to suggestions. But some shortcuts will reduce your standards.

- **Learn how to create challenge programs** from Dr. John Sullivan (San Francisco State University) at ourworld.compuserve.com/homepages/gately/ pp15js34.htm. Read about Peak Performance: *Aligning the Hearts and Minds of Your Employees* by Jon R. Katzenbach.

Leadership Tips

There are dozens of leadership gurus, business experts and motivational consultants to assist you in improving your people skills. Every major bookstore has an aisle full of the latest and greatest ways to "shape" people into great employees. The thousands of ideas espoused in these books and in the resources here won't be any good if you don't respect your employees first. As we discussed in "What Motivates People," some basic human needs must be met before you buy any inexpensive prizes or get out the clown suit! Below are more useful tips and resources for leading and motivating your team to success.

- **Learn how to manage and motivate all types of employees.** Learn how to manage teen workers from Teenage Work Force Solution at www.teenagework-forcesolutions.com/ teen_employees-seminars.htm; Gen X from consultant Judy Cox at www.media3pub.com/ usbank/articles/genx.html; older workers from Hard at Work at www.hardatwork.com/Stump/ME/ OlderWorkers.html; and Managing Older Workers from 50-Minute Books at www.50minutebooks.com; Hispanics with audiotapes from Bridgeworks.net at www.bridgeworks.net/audio.htm; and short-term workers from Hard at Work at www.hardatwork.com/ Stump/ME/ShortTerm.html.

- **Is poor performance your fault?** Find out from

Business Know How at www.businessknowhow.com/manage/poorperf1.htm.

- **Don't spend anything.** Learn cashless ways to motivate from BizTraining.com www.biztrain.com/motivation/stories/cashless.htm.

- **Try some of these books** on motivating employees: *1001 Ways to Energize Employees* by Bob Nelson and Kenneth H. Blanchard. *Recognizing and Rewarding Employees* by R. Brayton Bowen. *The X-Factor: Getting Extraordinary Results from Ordinary People* by Ross R. Reck, Ph.D. *From Turnover to Teamwork: How to Build and Retain a Customer-Oriented Foodservice Staff* by Bill Marvin. *Playing Games at Work: 52 Best Incentives, Contests and Rewards for the Hospitality Industry* by Phil Roberts and T. J. McDonald. *Coaching and Mentoring for Dummies* by Marty Brounstein.

Employee Policies

An employee manual addresses a wide variety of employment issues. A good manual explains:

ACTIVITY	EXAMPLES
Employer responsibilities	Performance reviews, complaint handling, payroll.
Employee benefits	Vacation, sick days, insurance.
Operational procedures	Clock in/out, check cashing.
Behavioral rules	Dress code, substance abuse, absenteeism.
Disciplinary/Termination	Specific procedures and grounds for action.
Employee agreement	Confirms acceptance and understanding of company policies.

- **Hire an expert to create your employee manual.** Companies like Literary Technologies, www.literarytechnologies.com and Personnel Policies, www.personnelpolicies.com, can handle everything from gathering information to printing. Or see the Employee Handbook Creator Guide from Atlantic Publishing at www.atlantic-pub.com.

- **Get expert advice.** Employee manuals can be considered contracts by the courts. An attorney should review your manual BEFORE you distribute it. The National Restaurant Association can help you with How to Write an Employee Manual at www.restaurant.org/business/howto/eemanual.cfm.

- **Get a signature.** Obtain a signature confirming they received a copy and accept responsibility for reading and complying with its contents. Some HR experts advise that you have employees read the manual immediately and return with questions.

- **Avoid legalese.** Your manual should be written in conversational English. Your employees need to understand it more than your lawyers do!

- **Address specifics.** For help in writing policies on important issues, check out the following Web sites and online articles: For dress codes (including tattoos, piercings) see Personnel Policy Service, Inc. at www.ppspublishers.com/dresscodepolicy2.htm. For workplace weapons policy see the State of Minnesota Department of Labor at www.doli.state.mn.us/vguideape.pdf. For the drug-free workplace policy from the U.S. Small Business Administration see www.dfwp.utsa.edu. Eliminate customer complaints, allergic reactions and conflicting smells with your great food. Fragrance information can be found at www.ameliaww.com/fpin/Devel.

- **Alcohol abuse.** Alcohol use and abuse in establishments selling alcohol can be a larger issue than for other businesses. In most states, you can be held liable for the actions of employees who consume alcohol provided by your business.

- **Watch your alcohol inventory.** The New York Times addresses alcohol theft at www.bevinco.com/spirits.htm.

Gone, But Not Forgotten

Employee absenteeism is technically an unscheduled failure to report to work. Because these events cannot be planned for, productivity and morale are immediately impacted and chaos can rein. Scheduled or not, absenteeism occurs for physical and emotional reasons. It is a barometer of employee morale and costs your business! Your first five steps in combating excessive absences should be to:

- **Calculate the cost of absenteeism to your business.** Use the calculator provided by Harris, Rothenberg International at www.harrisrothenberg.com/vc/vc-comp-abs.htm.

- **Invest these losses into prevention.**

- **Discover the true reason for the absence.** Benefits.org can guide you with their Attendance Management Program at www.benefits.org/interface/cost/absent2.htm.

- **Create an absenteeism policy.** Review tips and a policy sample at Business Owner's Toolkit Web site, www.toolkit.cch.com/text/P05_5325.asp.

- **Take proactive steps.** Employer-Employee.com addresses employer concerns and employee needs at www.employer-employee.com/absent.html.

Drug and Alcohol Problems

Drug- and alcohol-related issues cause U.S. companies over $100 billion annually. One in five workers report that they have had to work harder, redo work or cover for a coworker or have been put in danger or injured as a result of a fellow employee's drinking. Almost 68 percent of illegal drug users are employed either full- or part-time according to the National Institute on Drug Abuse. To learn more, read:

- ***Drug and Alcohol Abuse in the Workplace*** by the National Crime Prevention Council, www.ncpc.org/1wkdrugs.htm.

- ***Uncovering the Hidden Signs of Workplace Substance Abuse*** by the Department of Labor at www.dol.gov/asp/programs/drugs/workingpartners/uncover.htm.

Employee Problems

Disruptive behaviors, dishonesty, poor work performance and absenteeism are problems that create destructive ripples and affect your staff and business. One reason good employees leave is that management doesn't properly or promptly address problems with other employees. Good people want to work in an environment where professionalism, hard work, honesty and service are rewarded – not where the opposite exists by default! Here are a few tips on handling employee problems to keep productivity and morale high:

- **Don't bury your head.** Ostrich-style management is frequently based on an erroneous belief that you must keep the restaurant staffed at any cost. Ignoring problems could mean the only employees you'll be keeping are the problem ones!

- **Discourage gossip.** Gossip is always destructive and

workplace gossip can cause enormous employee stress and dissension.

- **Protect your employees.** You have a responsibility to provide a safe and secure environment. This includes sexual and religious harassment and workplace conflicts. Even seemly routine employee problems can transform a peaceful workplace into a scene of violence.

- **Don't let employees use the threat of quitting as a weapon.** This is a poor management style and gives others the impression that you're playing favorites.

- **Give "negative" feedback in private.** Workers often feel a bond with peers and consider management the "opposition." Keep disciplinary actions private to avoid fueling these beliefs.

- **Fit the punishment to the "crime."** Establish grounds for disciplinary action and termination in your personnel manual.

- **Manage employee conflict.** To learn how, see Management Association Program for Nonprofits' Conflict Management Guide at www.mapnp.org/ library/intrpsnl/conflict.htm. Get advice on handling problem employees from BusinessTown.com at www.businesstown.com/people/employees.asp.

- **Pay attention to employee stress.** Stress Directions can give you some valuable insights into the importance of monitoring and reducing employee stress at www.stressdirections.com.

- **Understand the legal issues relating to problem employees**. Attorneys Amy Delpo and Lisa Guerin can help with the book, *Dealing With Problem Employees: A Legal Guide.*

Disciplinary Action

Disciplining employees is an unpleasant duty for supervisors. But failing to do so undermines management and disrespects your other workers.

- **Act early before problems become severe.** *A Check-up for Under-Performing Employees* by Dave Anderson at Golden Nuggets Software at www.bss-gn.com/nl/july2000/art003.htm.

- **Be consistent and fair.** Video and workbooks to teach proper (legal) disciplining methods is available from Management Training Videos at www.management-trainingvideos.com.

- **Handle with care.** Union workers, employees covered by the American Disabilities Act (ADA) and others may be covered by contracts and/or laws that establish how you can discipline and terminate. We recommend that you have a labor attorney guide you through these issues.

- **Document well.** Business Owner's Toolkit offers comprehensive guidance on documenting disciplinary actions at www.toolkit.cch.com/text/P05_7230.asp.

- **Coach for improvement.** See *10 Keys for Successfully Coaching Employees* by Mark Campbell (article available at Society of Professional Consultants' site at www.spconsultants.org/articles/mcampbell.htm or the *Employee Development & Coaching Guide*) from Accel-Team www.accel-team.com/human_resources/coaching.html.

- **Make the "punishment" fit the crime.** Progressive discipline is common personnel practice. Many labor experts advise that this is the ONLY way to protect your business against possible wrongful termination claims and lawsuits. Also, hospitality workers' unions may spell out your disciplinary requirements in contracts. Read about its disadvantages at Business Owner's Tool Kit, www.toolkit.cch.com/text/ P05_7265.asp.

- **Terminate when warranted.** *When You Can Legally Fire Employees*, an All Business educational article at www.allbusiness.com/articles/content/HR_article24.asp, will help you make this critical decision.

Terminate Wisely

You owe it to your business and your other employees to remove disruptive, non-productive or insubordinate employees from your staff. Keeping "bad" employees affects your entire team's productivity. Below are additional resources.

- **National Restaurant Association addresses termination issues.** For how-to and legal issues, see www.restaurant.org/legal/law_termination.cfm. For tactful terminations, see www.restaurant.org/rusa/magArticle.cfm?ArticleID=423.

- **Be careful when firing a popular employee.** If the grounds are fair, your staff is probably more aware of the problems than you realize. Because the employee is well-liked, managers often hesitate to discipline and delay terminating the employee until the behavior becomes severe. This delay increases the stress among the remaining staff and undermines your authority. Don't ignore other performance problems, as this can fuel any claims of unfair treatment.

- **Build support.** Although you cannot share confidential information about employee terminations, you can build support within your staff and encourage them to pick up additional responsibilities while you restaff.

- **Investigation thoroughly.** You may even have to interview other employees. HRZone offers advice on this step at www.hrzone.com/topics/firing.html.

• **Be prepared for a negative reaction.** Even if you have been coaching and counseling the employee on their unacceptable behavior or inadequate performance, you should be prepared for an emotional response.

• **Terminate immediately** (without disciplinary action) when employee safety is an issue (conflicts, threats and violence), when employees are carrying contraband (drugs, weapons), when employees commit illegal acts (theft, embezzlement), or when employees are under the influence of alcohol or drugs.

Employee Turnover

With restaurant turnover rates running as high as 200 percent annually, no other personnel issue is as costly. Turnover increases your costs for employee searching, hiring and training. Restaffing and training can also cost your business thousands annually in productivity losses and customer service declines.

• **They'll always leave.** You'll never eliminate employee turnover. And, in fact, you don't really want to. Turnover is what brings you fresh faces, innovative methods, youthful exuberance, wisdom and experience, trendsetting ideas, and new skills. Your goal is to reduce it, manage it and transform it into new opportunities.

Why They Leave

You'll lose employees because of poor training, retirement, physical and mental health concerns, graduation, competition, poor wages/benefits, burnout, stress, transfers, poor attitudes, family needs, desire for personal growth, and death. Some are not in your control; however, you can positively influence many of these factors. Understanding why your employees leave is your first step to reducing turnover.

- **Listen and learn.** We don't just mean staff meetings or boss-to-employee lectures. Take time to ask and listen about their families, expectations and dreams.

- **Survey them.** Employee satisfaction surveys are one way to head off problems. See Business Research Lab at www.busreslab.com/consult/empsat.htm or Employee Surveys at www.employeesurveys.com.

- **Interview them.** Exit interviews are valuable information gathering opportunities. If you find that your departing employees aren't forthcoming, you might try hiring a consultant to follow-up with surveys, interviews or questionnaires. Financial incentives can improve your success rate and can pay off. To learn more about conducting exit interviews, visit Bill Marvin, The Restaurant Doctor at www.restaurantdoctor.com/articles/exit.html.

The Cost of Turnover

The National Restaurant Association puts the average cost of losing a minimum-wage hourly employee at $2,494 and a manager at $24,000. Using these statistics, a restaurant with 75 hourly employees and three managers, a 90-percent turnover rate translates into over $203,000 lost each year. With numbers like these, even small operations should "invest" in creating a work environment that provides stability, financial security and emotional support to its employees. Invest your time and money in retaining valued employees. To learn more about turnover costs:

- **Use the turnover calculator** at www.uwex.edu/ces/cced/publicat/turn.html to learn how turnover affects your business. These cost figures don't take into account the productivity and quality factors that indirectly impact customers, employees and your bottom line.

CHAPTER SIX

SCHEDULING YOUR STAFF

The Eight Basic Scheduling Steps

There are eight basic steps in the scheduling process:

- **Developing work production standards.** Calculate the amount of work (covers, meals, place settings) that an individual employee with a specific job (server, cook, dishwasher) is expected to accomplish in a set time period.

- **Plotting patterns of activity in various units of the operation.** Food service facilities usually have different patterns of activity during the day that require different levels of scheduling.

- **Forecasting levels of activity.** Shift, daily, weekly and monthly customer/sales cycles should be factored in. These can be broken down into quarter, half and hourly segments within each day.

- **Determining the number of workers and/or hours needed.** Divide the work production standards into the anticipated number of covers (customers) and the number of personnel required can be calculated.

- **Considering employee time and assignment requests.** Job assignments; skills, abilities and experience; scheduled absences, desired rotation; wage rates; and legal considerations such as hours for minors and overtime are all important considerations.

- **Approval by management after the schedule is written.** Evaluate by criteria such as labor cost per hour, customers served per hour or any other appropriate criteria.

- **Distributing approved schedule to employees.** Employee handouts, break room and office postings, Web site postings, e-mail broadcast and "call-in" systems are all ways to ensure staff members have ample notification of shift assignments.

- **Recapping and reviewing the historical schedules by management** to discover problems, explore solutions and improve processes.

Scheduling Truisms

Your goal is to complete all necessary work using the least number of labor hours possible while maintaining an outstanding level of service. It's better to start out under-staffed.

- **Establish a baseline for a minimally acceptable service level.** Then analyze how each additional worker impacts service quality and productivity. Remember, employees appreciate getting more help but become irritated when they "lose" help.

- **Absenteeism** will play havoc on your fine-tuned schedule on a regular basis. Controlling unplanned absences is critical to maintaining adequate productivity and service levels. See the section on "Absenteeism" for more information.

- **Good forecasting requires good data.** Historical and current data must be accurately gathered and easily assessable.

- **Outside factors,** such as seasonal demands, weather conditions, special events and competitive issues, are important forecasting issues.

- **You must understand your team's capabilities and capacities.** Consider individual skills and abilities to balance scheduling. People have active/sleep cycles and are more productive during specific times of the day. Some servers cope with noisy children better so schedule them during family times. Family needs create unplanned absences and distract workers. Whenever possible, you should consider these during scheduling. "Favoring" workers with families over singles is a discriminatory practice.

- **Overworking** (physically and emotionally) staff members can significantly lower productivity, increase absenteeism and escalate turnover rates. Frazzled employees are potential customer service nightmares. Inattentive service, inaccurate orders, spills and angry encounters lower your service quality and chase away customers. Tired employees can cut corners – increasing food safety problems, food waste, equipment and dishware damage, accidents and injuries.

- **Overstaffing** doesn't just inflate your payroll, it can decrease your overall productivity. Congested serving and kitchen areas makes everyone's job more difficult and lowers service quality.

- **You must balance quality and quantity.** A fast cook who makes mistakes and turns out sloppy meals is not up to your quality standards. A slow cook who turns out perfect meals is not up to the quantity standards.

Schedule Types and Patterns

There are different types of schedules that can be used in a food service operation.

- **Scheduling by production requirements for individual items.** Determine what has to be produced for the meal, period or day. You may include items that will be produced for future meals.

- **Scheduling by station production.** Items from the production schedule are assigned to a workstation (e.g., bakery, salads, etc.). Smaller operations may combine a production schedule and a station work guide.

- **Scheduling by staff coverage (individual schedules).** This provides coverage for the various units within the operation. Production schedules should be coordinated with individual scheduling. Dining room scheduling is based on the forecasted number of patrons divided by the work production standards of the dining room personnel.

There are three common scheduling patterns:

- **Block or stacked schedule.** Everyone on a shift starts and stops working at the same time. This makes it easier to check that everyone is present and on time and share common information. This works best for operations closed between meal times as customers aren't directly affected by a staff changes.

- **Staggered arrivals and departures.** Employee schedules correspond to the work pattern and customer flow. More efficient than block scheduling, as the number of employees gradually increases during the peak volume periods and decreases towards the end of the day.

- **Spanner shifts**. Overlapping coverage for a smooth transition between shift changes. Overlap times range from 30-60 minutes depending upon the job category and duties. It eliminates staff working past scheduled departure times to "finish up."

Other Possible Scheduling Methods

Forecasting can be difficult, especially for newer establishments without any historical data to draw from. This can cause scheduling inaccuracies that inflate your labor costs or result in substandard service. You'll find that unplanned events can directly impact your staffing requirements. There are other scheduling procedures to help you through unpredictable times. Below we'll discuss six ways you might consider. Although federal Wage & Hour law does not address these issues, you should be aware of union contracts, local labor practices, corporate policies and state laws that may govern your use of flexible scheduling practices. Meal and rest periods may also be mandated by your state even if workers are on the clock for less than 8 hours.

- **On-call scheduling.** Hourly employees remain at home until you call them into work. Quick response can be critical so employees can be given pagers or cell phones so they aren't "trapped" at home. Employees can rotate being on-call to give them additional free time without significantly affecting their paycheck. On-call periods would be scheduled like any other work duty. Trainees and new hires can be used for on-call coverage during probationary periods. Minimum hours may be mandated by union contracts and other labor practices.

- **Send home early scheduling.** The reverse of on-call scheduling, employees are sent home when work slows. With good forecasting and intelligent scheduling, this would typically be used for unusual circumstances, such as bad weather. Employees can rotate, draw straws or volunteer to go home early. Trainees and new hires (seniority) can be chosen.

- **Part-timers.** Schedule part-timers for additional coverage during peak periods and seasonal influxes. Post a roster of workers interested in part-time or temporary work. This can be a good choice for people seeking part-time work with exceptional flexibility. High school and college students who need to work around class schedules or during summer, spring and winter breaks, retirees who needing to supplement social security or mothers interested in working during school hours.

- **Split shifts.** Similar to part-timers but where employees would work multiple, non-consecutive mini-shifts totaling up to 40 hours a week. Employees clock out between scheduled work periods. Workers would cover specific meal periods or required prep and clean up times (before and after peak periods).

- **On-break schedules.** When it isn't practical to send someone home, you can put them on an extended break. A 30-minute off-the-clock break and employer-provided meal means you can deduct the cost of the meal against the minimum wage requirement and save half an hour of pay.

- **Short-term overtime.** Overtime is costly but sometimes necessary when unforeseen emergencies arise and short-term coverage is required. Beware of burnout and stress when employees are working extra hours to help out.

The Negative Impacts of Understaffing

Unskilled managers can be too zealous in keeping labor costs low. A shortage of workers and/or relying primarily on inexperienced, lower-paid workers will initially reduce your costs. However, the long-term impact on service, morale and productivity could mean a slow and painful death for your business. Below are some useful resources and ideas on how to measure whether your staffing levels are creating problems.

- **Ask your customers.** Tour the dining room throughout the meal, asking about their dining experience. Conduct customer service surveys. For information on surveys, visit The Business Research Lab at www.busreslab.com/consult/restcslg.htm or Mercantile Systems and Surveys at www.mercsurveys.com.

- **Hire a "mystery shopper."** Professionals visit your restaurant to gather info and report on your customer service. Check the Mystery Shopping Providers Association at www.mysteryshop.org, 972-406-1104, for a local consultant.

- **Employees suffer.** You risk losing your most productive employees, as they will probably be the ones working longer hours. Overworked employees can quickly become unhappy and unproductive employees. Some employees won't complain; they'll just lose their incentive to work hard – then they'll leave. Others will develop a disruptive attitude – then they'll leave.

- **Costs soar.** Instead of saving money, you'll be spending more through lost productivity and lost customers! Other potential liabilities could be costly. As detailed in *Nation's Restaurant News* (July 20, 1998), cumulative fatigue can become a financial burden. A McDonald's restaurant was held responsible for $400,000 in personal injury damages after an employee, who had worked three consecutive shifts in 24 hours then fell asleep at the wheel, was involved in a serious collision.

- **Business declines.** How long customers will wait varies from establishment to establishment. Customer expectations during a workday lunch are significantly different than at a leisurely resort. In our fast-food nation, waiting is a major issue for diners. Customers will only put up with slow service for so long.

The Negative Impact of Overstaffing

Having too many people on hand can affect your bottom line in more ways than just wasting your payroll budget!

- **Don't forget Parkinson's Law:** "Work expands so as to fill the time available for its completion." If you give someone two hours to do a one-hour job, it will take two hours. Or, if two people are scheduled to do a one-person job, it will take both of them to get it done.

- **Poor work habits and attitudes will rise as employees slow down.** Employees will resist an increase in their workload after being overstaffed for a while. They will have adapted their performance levels to a lower productivity standard. They will even feel overworked and find it difficult to "speed up."

- **Unneeded workers with idle time become distractions.** Water cooler chit-chat begins to interfere with customer needs. The atmosphere becomes too relaxed and service declines due to the resulting apathy.

- **Physical and mental fatigue becomes an issue** because of boredom and time-wasting habits. Morale drops because management must eventually reduce their labor costs. But before they do, tips will suffer which also creates motivational problems.

Scheduling Tips and Hints

We've put together some useful scheduling tips, hints and resources:

- **Develop a manpower plan to determine hiring needs.** Restaurantville.com tells you how to calculate whether you need to increase your staff at www.restaurantville.com/sc/hr/recruiting/needs.cfm.

- **Study your volume.** Schedule labor to match volume needs (level of activity).

- **Study the level of activity breakdowns by area.** For

example, kitchen help needed before the busy period (9-1), waitstaff during the busy period (11-2) and cleaning after (12-3).

- **Remember that different work units have different patterns of activity throughout the day.** Normally, activity is highest in the kitchen before it is in the serving areas. The dishwashing units' activity peak may be 15-45 minutes after the serving area peaks.

- **Schedule according to your customer flow.** You need more employees on hand during peak times, and less employees when you have fewer customers.

- **Plan for shift changes to minimize service disruptions.** Take into consideration the layout of your establishment and the total duties of each position.

- **Employees should be given enough flexibility to ensure that transitions are handle smoothly** and tasks completed to the customers' satisfaction. But set some limits to keep overtime in check. Check out Labor Wizard at www.laborwizard.com for useful tools and ideals.

Computerized Scheduling

Restaurants of all sizes can successfully implement computerized employee-scheduling systems and software. Employee scheduling can be handled by a Web site, an uncomplicated Windows® program, or linked directly to "time clocks." Below are a few sources for computerized scheduling:

- **Optimal Solutions** at www.optimal-solutions.com. They offer online solutions that run through your browser and desktop programs.

- **aSchedule for Restaurants** at www.aschedule.com.

The program can automatically calculate your labor costs per cover and has an "Overtime Alert." Two versions are available for small or multi-store operations.

- **Asgard Systems Inc.** at www.asgardsystems.com. The "Time Tracker" system also keeps track of vacation time, sick time, etc. It can review past activity and prepare payroll data.

- **Restaurant Technology, Inc.** at www.internetrti.com. Management, scheduling and accounting software for the food service industry.

- **Staff Schedule** at www.staffscheduling.com is a free Web-based scheduling program and can be accessed by management and employees from any Web-accessible computer to set and check work schedules.

- **Open Wave at www.open-wave.com** offers various Web- and PC-based programs.

- **Epicurus.** Scheduling and other food-professional software are reviewed at Epicurus at www.epicurus.com/pros/software.html.

- **Explore software that captures data directly from your time clock.** These programs automatically track employee hours, let you know if someone is late or early, warn you of possible overtime, and even send the information directly to your payroll software.

CHAPTER SEVEN

PRODUCTIVITY

Prodcutivity

Profits are simply the difference between what you sell and what it costs you to sell it! To increase profits, you can increase sales or decrease costs. Your serving staff should all be trained to "sell" more – larger tickets lower your cost per cover. However, an extra $150 per shift doesn't increase profits by $150. After costs and taxes, you might be lucky to net $20! But saving $150 by operating more efficiently increases your bottom line by $150. Improved productivity can be defined as working smarter, not harder, to achieve more. To increase your staff's productivity, changes can be:

- **Simple.** Buying extra trashcans.

- **Complex.** Commissioning work-motion studies.

- **Free.** Overcoming poor work habits.

- **Costly.** Remodeling the entire kitchen.

- **Physical.** Building a facility with no steps.

- **Psychological.** Creating an "ownership" attitude.

Productivity is Also a Quality Goal

If the quality of your food and customer service declines, you have hurt your business, not helped it. The most important factor in improving productivity is smart management.

- **Don't compromise your quality standards.** A change that noticeably lowers your quality will also noticeably lower your sales! Beware of changes done for the sake of "efficiency" that cause employee morale to decline.

- **Invest in your businesses' productivity.** Invest in training. Well-trained employees are happier, more productive, less prone to job stress and less likely to be lured away by your competition. Or, invest in equipment that pays for itself in labor-savings. Or, invest in a worker-friendly building. Make it easier for your staff to do their jobs with proper ergonomics and well-designed rooms.

Productive People

There are three basic ways to make employees more "cost-effective." First, get more work from the employees you have in the same number of hours. Second, get the same amount of work from fewer employees in the same number of hours. Third, get the same amount of work from fewer employees in fewer hours. To help your employees reach their productivity potential, we've outlined some business concepts and suggestions on implementing them.

- **Make it important.** Being profitable is important to everyone! It's important to your customers, your staff, your management, your community and you – the owner. Getting everyone to share this never-ending goal is your first step in directing people to be more efficient. Employees that see a direct correlation between their work performance, the customer's satisfaction and your restaurant's success are going to work harder.

- **Don't waste a minute.** Have time cards initialed by the manager on duty upon arrival and departure. You'll know exactly when the employees arrive and start to work, but your manager also gets the chance to check the employees' appearance. If there are special instructions to be given to an employee, the manager doesn't have to go looking for anyone. At the end of each shift, the manager has an opportunity to thank the employee and privately address problems.

- **Listen to your employees.** No one knows better what it takes to improve a job than the person doing it. The most valuable "boss" has the ability to listen.

- **Always follow up somehow.** The quickest way to create unhappy employees is to "forget" to handle suggestions and complaints. When asking for input, remember that it always requires some "output" by management. This doesn't mean you have to implement every one or "solve" every complaint – it means that you take them seriously and act accordingly. Your actions tell your employees that their ideas and opinions have value!

- **Make it clear.** Detail tasks in writing. Write job descriptions and break down tasks into simple steps. This will help you set time and performance standards and make it easier to train employees. Plus, it lets employees know what needs to be done.

- **Set production standards.** Set goals to benchmark performance expectations and encourage employees to find ways to do their jobs better, faster and easier. Bonuses can be offered for exceeding standards.

- **Give employees benchmarks and guidelines for improvement.** Don't just set minimum standards. Tell them what they can do to be a top performer! And then reward them.

- **Assign tasks based on skill level and ability.** Match the job with the right person. Tasks should be assigned to the lowest-paid employee capable of successfully handling the job.

- **Share information regularly and consistently.** Good communication is critical to creating a productive service team. Schedule daily orientation meetings to review specials and menu changes; set sales goals and incentives; review procedural changes; and address potential problems. Schedule weekly meetings to recap your restaurant's production and employee performance. Thank and reward people! Address customer problems and complaints. Schedule monthly or quarterly meetings with your full staff. These team-building sessions are where you reinforce good behavior and attitudes and develop strong bonds.

- **Reinforce your message** with handouts, diagrams and illustrations. Post information on an employee-only Web page and break room bulletin boards.

- **Stimulate, but don't stifle.** Some employees are "naturally" productive. Their personal work ethic and positive attitude make them self-motivated and productive. Sometimes it can seem as if these are "problem" employees, as they tend to be more independent and headstrong. Your job is to harness and direct their energies without stifling them.

- **Make it worth it.** Create productivity incentives. Beyond rewarding your most productive employees with higher wages, consider bonus programs and profit sharing to make everyone personally connected to and responsible for productivity.

- **Consider sharing ownership.** Studies have shown that when employees own a "piece of the pie," they increase their productivity. This could be accomplished literally by creating employee ownership programs, forming partnerships, offering share options or giving stock bonuses, or figuratively by linking pay structures and bonuses to profitability. To learn more about employee ownership options, visit the Foundation for Enterprise Development and The Beyster Institute for

Entrepreneurial Employee Ownership at www.fed.org/allabout/allabout.htm.

- **Create a reward program.** You can offer fun prizes monthly for the best laborsaving suggestion. Or, go all out and create a "share-the-wealth" program where employees are rewarded a percentage of the documented savings.

- **Make it easier.** Watch your employees at work. Silent observation can reveal inefficiencies in your system. Mentally break down their activities into small segments to see where you can add laborsaving equipment, rearrange the work center or save steps between work areas.

- **Train and supervise.** Untrained employees are not working up to their potential. Unsupervised employees won't do their job quickly and accurately unless they clearly know what their job is! The chapter "Employee Training" provides you with more in-depth information.

- **Reduce employee stress and fatigue.** Working people harder will increase productivity but only to a point! Employee burnout is 60-percent emotional and 40-percent physical.

- **Cross-train and rotate staff.** Monotony and repetition can "burn out" employees and decrease their output. Changing duties can provide an emotional and/or physical lift.

- **Make it last.** Build in checks and balances to see that shortcuts aren't being taken which compromise your performance, quality or safety standards. Assign team leaders to supervise implementation of productivity changes.

- **Create a follow-up plan** to verify that employees

haven't fallen back into old habits. Don't let turnover degrade good habits and efficient procedures.

Streamlined Tasks

Manufacturing productivity experts can spend hours analyzing what's the fastest and most efficient method for inserting Part A into Part B. You should be looking at your daily operations from the same point of view: How can we do it better? To follow are some suggestions to get you started in reviewing tasks and establishing better procedures and methods.

- **There usually isn't just one "right" way to do something.**

- **It's easier to replace a bad habit with a good one** than to try to "break" it!

- **Target specific activities for time and performance studies** one at a time. Don't overload yourself and your staff by trying to improve EVERYTHING at once!

- **Tackle the obvious first.** A few positive changes can stimulate your team to work together to find other areas for improvement.

- **Analyze production standards on a daily basis.** It takes some time and analysis to determine standards, but it's worth the effort. See the chapter "Setting Standards" for more information.

- **Advance planning is the key to controlling costs.** Plan production activities in advance. Group together like activities in specific timeframes to minimize clean up.

- **Review your menu choices.** Are you selling enough of a specific item to warrant the labor required to prep, prepare and serve it? Will altering a recipe slightly allow you to do more advance prep? Does purchasing fully prepped ingredients or pre-processed entrées cost less than handling it in-house?

- **Provide less service.** If your restaurant style lends itself to self-serve salad bars, buffets and self-bussing, you can cut your staffing needs and your labor costs. When reviewing the cost/benefit analysis, be certain to consider the cost of equipment, shrinkage/waste and customer perception. Remember, many people eat out because they are waited on.

- **Make use of new, more efficient equipment.** Conveyer-style dishwashers can eliminate a part-time dishwasher. See our chapter on Labor Savers for more information on productivity-enhancing equipment and tools.

Work Smarter, Not Harder

To unlock productivity in your team:

- **Read a book.** *Work Smarter, Not Harder! The Service That Sells! Workbook for Foodservice*, available from Atlantic Publishing at www.atlantic-pub.com.

- **Hire an efficiency consultant** like Peggy Duncan, www.duncanresource.com.

- **Learn how Pal's did it.** This Tennessee fast-food chain, www.palsweb.com, won the prestigious 2001 Malcolm Baldrige Quality Award, www.nist.gov/public_affairs/pals.htm.

- **Give small, unexpected rewards.** A job well done should never go unnoticed. An inexpensive reward like a quick-pick lottery ticket or movie pass.

- **Conduct memorable meetings.** Routine meetings become routine. Keep employees on their toes with humor, silly costumes, magicians, humorous training videos and other attention-getters. To learn how to have fun meetings, see EffectiveMeetings.com at www.effectivemeetings.com/meetingplanning/fun/meetinglite.asp or Patricia Fripp at www.fripp.com/art.makefun1.html. You can also laugh with Monty Python member John Cleese in training videos from Training ABC at www.trainingabc.com/johncleese.htm.

- **Work ahead.** The more activities you can combine before serving times, the more prep labor you'll save.

Adopt Technology

The importance of technology to the restaurant industry cannot be understated. For an industry with steady but unspectacular growth of 1-3 percent annually since 1991, technology offers one of the few opportunities for cutting costs, improving efficiency and affecting the bottom line. Restaurateurs have been slow to adopt technological advances for a wide variety of reasons from not enough buying power to the feeling restaurants should be "run" by people, not computers. The broad acceptance of computers in our daily lives, from ATMs to the Internet, has taken away much of the apprehension. The food service industry began looking to technology for cost-cutting assistance in the 1990s. From 1992 to 1997, computer-related expenses more than doubled in our industry. "Early adopters" supported the evolution of technologically based advancements making them more user-friendly, dependable and affordable.

The right computer system can help you reduce both labor and food costs. Computers can reduce your paperwork, allowing your managers to spend their time managing people instead of paper. The efficiency of computerized systems can also help you to maximize your people resources through better scheduling and communications.

- **Invest for today and tomorrow, but don't overbuy.** Your equipment should meet your current needs and be able to handle your growth. Conversely, don't overbuy "just in case." If you can stand in the corner and see your entire establishment, then your needs are much less complex than if your establishment has 300 seats spread over two or three floors.

- **Hire an expert.** Unless you've got a lot of time on your hands or are already a computer whiz, you can actually SAVE money by hiring an expert to research, purchase and implement complex systems.

- **Establish what you want to accomplish BEFORE you buy.** This will help you focus on solutions and not toys! It's easy to get caught up in a salesperson's pitch and forget your objective.

Other Ways to Save Labor

- **Use disposables.** If the ecological concerns of disposables aren't a concern, disposables can be a labor-saver when it comes to those nasty clean ups.

- **Label and color code.** Create a color-code system to quickly identify items at a glance. Colored labels can help people return items to their proper storage area or let them know if it needs to be refrigerated. See www.dissolveaway.com.

- **Use napkin rings.** Build wrapped napkin/silverware sets ahead of time to save table-setting time. You'll also reduce storage handling and rewashing. Add your restaurant logo for a personal touch. Bands are available from ColorKraft at www.colorkraft.com, 866-382-4730.

- **Use Griptite™ serving trays.** Available from local suppliers, these metal trays have a non-slip surface for easier carrying. The 31-inch oval tray can hold 8 **105** dinners!

- **Eliminate clutter.** Clutter is defined as anything that has no immediate use or value. Everything else should be tossed or properly stored! Hire an organizational expert to review your storage systems and suggest ways to reduce handling costs.

- **Eliminate pot and pan cleanup with PanSaver,** available at www.atlantic-pub.com. PanSaver is a high-temperature (400° F/204° C) material designed as a commercial pot and pan liner that keeps pans clean and can be used to store leftovers.

- **Use pre-prepared products.** There's almost no ingredient that doesn't come prepped, portion-controlled or prepared for reheating. Not all are good candidates for your restaurant, but many can be incor-porated into your food offerings, without any noticeable quality decline.

- **Review your menu for pre-prepared possibilities.** Food that is eaten in its most natural state – washed, cut and ready to serve, like fruit and vegetables – is an obvious choice. Bread products that are proof and bake- or brown-and-serve are another option. Tea and lemonade concentrates are very common and taste better than powdered versions.

CHAPTER EIGHT

PRODUCTIVE BUILDINGS

Building in Efficiency

In building or remodeling your restaurant, you have the opportunity to build in labor-savers. From the building's infrastructure to the decorative touches, you should review the form, function and material choices for potential time savings. Your restaurant is your factory and, like any good factory, it needs to be designed with your workers and their productivity in mind. This chapter will explore construction, design and decorating issues and how they affect labor costs.

Site Selection

- **Select land/buildings with sufficient exterior space for waste/recycling activities and deliveries.** You'll need good access, wide doors and ample ramps. Avoid sites that would require time-consuming hand offloading. If you'll be receiving palleted goods; be certain you'll be able to accommodate a small forklift and/or lift trucks.

- **Be careful when considering retrofitting buildings.** Buildings that weren't originally built as restaurants can pose some real challenges. Carrying a heavy tray up a small stairway or dozens of small isolated rooms will increase your servers' workload. Inadequate kitchen space or inconvenient storage can significantly slow your kitchen productivity.

- **Hide the wires!** Not only are exposed wires unsightly, they can also be potential safety hazards.

- **Deaden, mask or enhance sounds.** Excessive noise creates stress, increases fatigue and causes headaches.

- **Create a building that promotes productivity and safety.** Failing to properly address cleanliness, safety, workflow and ergonomic issues can put your customers, employees and business at risk.

- **When making construction and design choices, don't forget:**
  - Suitable work areas that eliminate potential cross-contamination.
  - Ample storage promotes good food-handling procedures and eliminates cluttered floors.
  - Ample lighting in common areas, workstations and "danger zones" to minimize accidents.
  - Proper drainage in wet areas (prep, restrooms) to prevent slip-and-fall injuries.
  - Appropriate non-slip or slip-resistant flooring material in high traffic and wet areas.

Select Materials That Do the Work

Some materials are obviously easier to clean, like cold-hard plastic. But unless you're building a kid-proof joint, your restaurant probably needs some softer, warmer touches to make it feel inviting. Your goal should be to incorporate as many easy-to-clean-and-maintain materials as possible. Here are some practical ideas for easy-care building materials. Entrances, waiting areas, dining rooms and restrooms can all benefit from materials that do the work!

- **Determine the area's "dirt" level.** The more potential dirt, the more important your material and color choices become. Front entrances and entries must be scrubbable, non-skid surfaces. Add mats inside and out to "catch" water, mud, sand and tar. Rent mats for more savings. Restrooms must be able to withstand heavy-duty cleaners, disinfectants and HOT water. In dining areas, select carpets/flooring that won't show footprints and crumbs.

- **Use color, texture and patterns to "hide" dirt and wear.** Make certain normal wear and tear (shoe scuffs, carpet wear, high-heel damage) and daily activities aren't visual negatives.

- **Seal surfaces whenever possible.** Porous materials, like your concrete walk and wood floors, should be professionally sealed to reduce stains and cleaning times.

- **Explore "self-cleaning" materials and products,** such as Self-Cleaning Glass from Pilkington Activ™, www.activglass.com or PPG Industries' Sunclean™, www.ppg.com/gls_sunclean. Bathrooms can feature automated public toilets from Exceloo, www.automatic-toilets.com. You may want to look into self-cleaning air cleaners from Peak Pure Air, www.peakpureair.net/aqe.htm.

- **Choose commercial-grade building materials.** Many building products have "industrial" grades that are designed for heavy-use environments. Be sure to read the warranty. Some building products have shorter warranty periods and/or limited coverage for commercial applications.

- **Look for materials/products that have antimicrobial agents** to prohibit microorganism growth. These shorten cleaning times by inhibiting the growth of bacteria, spores and molds. To learn more, visit Abiotics Online at www.geocities.com/hotsprings/6869/industrial.htm.

Healthy Environments

Healthy environments are productive environments. On-the-job injuries, workplace stress and unhealthy atmospheres are significant factors in high absenteeism and employee turnover. Your goal should be to create a pleasant work environment that minimizes employee stress, protects their health and promotes safety.

Ergonomics

Ergonomics is the study and engineering of human physical interaction with spaces and objects during activities. A prep area that requires workers to repeatedly stretch across to reach ingredients or a broiler unit that only very tall workers can safely reach is "poor" ergonomics. Good ergonomics, such as well-fitting tables and comfortable chairs, can also enhance your diners' experience. Here are some valuable tips to help you "engineer" your restaurant to work well with people.

- **Create mini-work stations** where all necessary food, utensils and prep spaces are close at hand.

- **Eliminate excessive bending, lifting and reaching** while encouraging proper prep and storage procedures.

- **Provide stools or chairs to give backs and feet a rest,** if the work being done doesn't require standing.

- **Make certain your tools and equipment weren't designed for only men.** Although more and more women are donning toques, tools and equipment haven't necessarily been redesigned to accommodate their shorter frames or differing physical characteristics.

- **Provide stable, heavy-duty work ladders** for accessing top shelves and deep storage units.

- **For left-handed employees,** purchase a supply of special tools and utensils.

- **Arrange seating to minimize steps** and reduce cross-traffic patterns.

- **Make a point to minimize your guests' exposure** to glare, drafts and noisy areas, and create easy entrances and exits.

- **Choose fixtures and equipment that can be easily moved** from work area to work area when needed.

- **Protect employees from injury by placing heavy items closest to waist height as possible.** Provide sturdy stepstools, ladders and rolling carts nearby. Except for rarely accessed areas, keep shelving shallow enough for easy reach.

The Air We Breathe

Healthy air is a business and moral concern that impacts restaurants legally and fiscally. "Poor air" contributes directly to employee absenteeism and workers' compensation claims. Many communities have rigid air emission and work environment regulations relating to proper ventilation, wood burning, grease and smoke. Unpleasant odors also contribute to "poor" air quality.

- **Physically separate smoking and non-smoking dining areas** and/or direct airflow away from non-smoking tables. Ban employee smoking in the kitchen, dining room and bar. Visit the Phillip Morris USA's Options Web site at www.pmoptions.com, dedicated to indoor air quality issues. You'll also find free assessment tools and an HVAC referral service.

- **Indoor air.** Wood-burning ovens, charbroilers, fryers and "sealed" buildings can also create unhealthy or unpleasant air conditions. Indoor air quality requires bringing sufficient outdoor air in, properly filtering the outdoor and recirculated air and directing airflow.

- **Improve indoor air quality** by installing a whole-building air cleaner/filtration system that also reduces airborne particles and dust. Also, check for radon, mold spores and biological dangers when converting older or long-vacant buildings. Read what the EPA says about indoor air quality at www.epa.gov/iaq/pubs/insidest.html. Be aware of unhealthy emissions from carpeting, paint and cleaning products. Sick Building Syndrome is explained at the National Safety Council site at www.nsc.org/ehc/indoor/sbs.htm.

Productive Environments

The layout of your establishment may be costing you money. Wasted movement is wasted time, which is a waste of your labor dollars.

- **Rearrange the work area.** The fewer steps your people have to take, the faster they can do their job.

- **Review your walkways and halls.** Have room for employees to move without bumping into others.

- **Study how your staff moves through the active and passive work areas.** Watch the traffic patterns. Do people have to stop to let others pass? Do they have to circle a dining room to get to the kitchen?

- **Increase productivity by creating three types of storage: active, back up and long-term.** Active storage is accessed repeatedly throughout the day and should be located closest to the active work area. Backup storage is used to refill (bulk) items for active areas and items used occasionally during one week. It should be located further from the active work area but easily accessible. Long-term storage is for nonperishable special-use and seasonal items. Locate it in an out-of-reach, less accessible area.

- **Eliminate unnecessary bending, stooping and reaching.** Simple, low-tech innovations can cut costs too. Try putting a shelf above the prep table for condiments. No turning or reaching. The preparer doesn't have to move to finish the plate. Read about designing a faster kitchen at Brew Pub magazine, brewpubmag.com/20mar/feature.html.

Beautiful and Carefree

Without interior decorating, you'd be serving meals in a warehouse. The beautiful touches you add to make the environment more attractive, more entertaining or more relaxing should also be practical and low maintenance. Decorative items shouldn't get in the way of good service or create work obstacles for servers. Here are several suggestions on how to keep your restaurant beautiful:

- **Rent greenery.** Your staff won't have to worry about regular care, plant rotation and seasonal updates.

- **Install quick-connect water valves/faucets** to water interior and exterior plants and trees. Access to water will make after-hours mopping and hosing quicker.

- **Install plenty of electrical, phone and sound system outlets.** No crawling under tables and over cabinets to plug in something.

- **Incorporate skylights, light tubes and windows to bring in more natural lights.** Studies show natural light increases productivity and reduces stress.

- **Explore full-spectrum lighting** (which reportedly makes people feel healthier) for work areas.

- **Make it easier for spur-of-the-moment room changes** with chairs that are easy to move, stack and store.

Choose round table tops in various sizes and separate legs/stands to mix and match. Utilize divider doors, screens and walls on rollers/casters/wheels.

- **Eliminate tablecloths.** Placemats take less time for setup. Or, if your restaurant theme is very informal – go bare! Tame table toppers. Don't overload the table slowing down setup and bussing.

Traffic and Workflow

A well-designed restaurant makes it easier and faster to serve meals. Improper workflow and poor traffic patterns mean thousands of wasted steps and movements every day. Analyzing your layout and equipment needs from the viewpoint of the user will increase productivity, decrease employee stress and injuries and improve your customers' service. To follow are some areas of traffic within your restaurant and how you might eliminate excess steps and waiting while increasing productivity.

- **Restrooms.** Place restrooms at the front of the restaurant to minimize traffic around the kitchen.

- **Hire a traffic/workflow expert.** A food service consultant specializing in traffic analysis and workflow streamlining can help you maximize your space while improving employee productivity.

- **Listen to your staff.** Service personnel, chefs and assistants with the hands-on experience can help you create layouts which help them respond quicker and improve morale.

- **Make the self-service counter easy to access.** Allow 4.5 feet for counter workers and 2.5 feet for back bar workers. Be certain trays, bins and service carts can fit between aisles and counter sides.

- **Help your servers and busperson.** Table layout can affect the speed diners are served and tables are cleared. If faster service is your goal, make certain servers aren't battling your table placement. Don't use fussy tablecloths and napkins, and make sure all surfaces can be cleaned quickly and efficiently.

- **Diagram the room.** Seeing where every table and workstation is placed in relationship to each other, and how they relate to the active food prep areas and kitchen, will help you eliminate unnecessary steps, cross-traffic and backtracking. Some designers can create helpful diagrams detailing the number of steps between tables and work areas. Or, try floor planner software. You can find information at OnTheRail.com, www.ontherail.com/site/news/floorplanner.asp.

- **Place banquet and large party areas closest to the kitchen** to improve service and food delivery times.

- **Enhance communication to reduce steps and speed service.** Centrally located or multiple-station POS equipment. Even more efficient is handheld order-entry systems that allow the waitstaff to move directly to the next customer. Use vibrating pagers and two-way radios to signal that tables are cleared or meals are ready.

- **Determine the activities your staff will be doing in the dining room** and at tableside. Plus, make certain staff can rearrange tables quickly and easily to accommodate the party's size.

Front-of-the-House Support Stations

Realistically, not all food prep and service work can be accomplished behind closed doors. To do so, would exhaust your waitstaff unnecessarily, slow down your service and create a workflow nightmare in the back-of-the-house.

The front-of-the-house may have a reception to meet and greet, take reservations and assign customers to servers. It would also have a cashier area to receipt meal payments, process credit card charges and sell retail items. A food service area for beverage centers, salad prep and dessert service may also be practical. Finally, dinnerware and utensil storage with a place for setups, additional napkins and specialty utensils can be helpful. Depending upon your restaurant layout, service methods, etc., some workstations may have multiple functions.

- **Don't forget to build in floor drains,** use scuff-resistant baseboards and add casters to equipment that must be moved for quick cleaning.

- **Reduce lifting and carrying** with mobile carts and rolling waste receptacles. Also, use antifatigue mats and non-slip flooring.

- **Use properly aimed task lighting** to avoid glare while allowing staff full visibility of the work surface.

- **Separate "wet" and "dry" tasks to avoid damage,** food contamination and electrical accidents. Incorporate hand and/or utility sinks whenever possible to save steps and promote cleanliness.

- **Provide ample counter space** below pass-throughs to add garnishes, verify orders and fill trays.

- **Consider incorporating a small (and quiet) under-counter glasswashe**r for thorough cleanup of critical tools and utensils.

Back-of-the-House – Your "Factory"

Too many people, too little space, too much work to get done in too short of a time. Sounds like a busy restaurant! Good traffic patterns and workflow make it easier for your chef and support staff to be productive.

- **Add traffic aisles.** Thirty inches is the minimum to allow traffic to move around the kitchen without interfering with active workspace. Be certain aisles are wide enough for mobile carts. Heavy traffic areas or aisles with workers on each side may require 48 inches or more.

- **Add extra doors for direct bar access.** Concentrate on straight-line production whenever possible.

- **Install separated kitchen access doors.** Separate doors should be 2-feet apart. Doors should only swing one way with large, clear, unbreakable windows in each. Clearly mark the doors – IN or OUT – on each side. Doors should be at least 42-inches wide. If separate doors aren't possible, use double-swinging doors (at least 84 inches total).

Employee Energy Boosters

- **Create rest areas.** Rest areas for employees should consist of something more than a back step. A peaceful area is a great way to rejuvenate employees and let them know important they are.

- **Don't overlook music in the kitchen and staff areas.** Music has proven to enhance productivity and reduce stress. Just make certain that it doesn't overwhelm normal voice level conversation.

- **Provide employee-only restrooms.** Employees will be able to feel more relaxed and get in and out quicker.

- **Create a covered employee-only area outside.** A bit of sun can be a great refresher. Also, smokers have a private area to smoke even during bad weather.

Kitchen Design

Good kitchen design is an art and a science. Hire a talented consultant to balance space limitations, safety issues, food prep needs and budgets without sacrificing food quality, productivity and your staff's sanity! Here are some suggestions on how you might make your kitchen layout work for your chef and support staff.

- **Know "what you'll serve"** (raw ingredients and prepared foods) and "how you'll serve it" to determine your prep, assembly, storage and serving needs.

- **Break your kitchen activities into self-contained workstations** where ingredients, tools, equipment and supplies are within easy reach.

- **Include plenty of waste receptacles.** Divide by type of waste if you will be implementing recycling programs.

- **Create work triangles.** Triangle or diamond layouts give quick access to prep tables, sinks and cooking equipment. Straight-line layouts work best for assembly-line style prep and cooking where more than one person participates.

- **Draw out traffic maps** to minimize unnecessary steps, crisscrossing paths.Then locate your cooking and final prep areas near dining areas to shorten kitchen trips.

- **Allow for ample open space.** People need to pass, carts need to be rolled, shelving needs to be moved, buckets need to be wheeled and trays need to be lifted.

- **Place your volume cooking areas towards the back of the kitchen** and your to-go order needs nearest dining areas. Production that requires little tending shouldn't take up precious high-activity space.

Labor-Saving Equipment

In a restaurant you are starting with raw material, creating a finished product and supplying it straight to the consumer, all on the same premises. From start to finish, machinery can help your employees to do their job faster. However, restaurants don't just sell food. They sell service, convenience and entertainment. It can be a mistake to replace people with self-service machines in some environments. You must balance your profit needs with your customers' expectations. From simple, little items that save a minute here and there to fully computerized and integrated kitchens, there is a plethora of equipment available to help you cut your costs and enhance your service. Here are helpful resources and practical ideas for every area of your operation.

- **Spending $10,000 on equipment could pay for itself in less than a year.** Equipment covered by IRS Code Section 179 (100-percent deductible in acquisition year) that eliminates one minimum-wage employee saves you thousands over the equipment's life.

- **Consider the equipment's length of service** and maintenance costs when calculating your savings.

- **Understand your customers' expectations.** Self-service is fine for fast food and family restaurants, but are a poor idea when people want to be waited on.

- **Test equipment with staff before buying.** Many distributors and local utility companies operate full test kitchens for demo purposes. Certainly an experienced factory rep can easily operate the stove, but if it is hard to operate or difficult to understand, it won't make things easier for your people.

- **Don't overbuy.** Do you need all those features? Or would a more basic model suit your needs?

- **Take time to train.** Many manufacturers or distributors offer training for your staff. Don't be afraid to ask for support.

- **Make certain it's easy to clean.** Prep and cooking timesavings can be wiped out if the equipment or tool takes too long to clean.

Front-of-the-House Labor Savers

Equipment, fixtures, furniture and decorative items are all potential labor-savers. Yes, even a chair can save you time if it's quick to clean, easy to move and convenient to store.

- **Create a communication station for your receptionist** by including a multi-line phone system, fax machine, POS system, guest and server paging and computer reservation systems. Don't forget network and Web access to monitor online reservations and food-to-go orders. Video camera systems can also help in seating patrons in larger or multi-story establishments.

- **Explore computer reservation and customer data systems.** Computerized reservation systems range from simple scheduling software for $150 to complex systems for $5,000 that can track your valued patrons' personal preferences and contact information. To learn more visit JCR System at www.jcrsystems.com/rsvip.htm or MicroCafe at www.microcafe.net for Reservation Pro.

- **Move some reservation functions to the Web.** Your Webmaster can assist you with scheduling via your Web site or you can use directory-style sites or three-party services. In major cities, you can list your restaurant on Web sites like Open Table at www.opentable.com and Food Line at www.foodline.com. For $54.95, CyberWhiz, www.cyberwiz.com, will host your reservations on the Web with SimpleREZ or you can purchase standalone applications.

Communication Systems

- **Wireless headsets** can save millions of steps a day by connecting your front-of-the-house staff with your bar and kitchen staff. Combined with a POS system, wireless technology can speed service and improve communications – even in noisy kitchen environments. To learn more about wireless communications, contact HM Electronics, www.hme.com, for a variety of wireless systems and pagers. Panasonic, www.panasonic.com/pos/ultraplextxt.htm, offers complete license-free 900MHz systems.

- **Silent pagers.** Hand waving, finger snapping and whistling for a server are a thing of the past. Never again will your customers be frustrated by an "invisible server." Silent pagers are the high-tech solution. One-button pagers are placed on the table. If the customer needs anything, they simply press the button. The appropriate waitperson is notified instantly and silently. A glance at the vibrating personal pager lets them know exactly which table needs their attention, no matter where in the building they may be. Pagers can also be used to let diners know their table is ready (even if they have wandered to the mall next door), signal a busy busperson or let the manager know they are needed tableside. JTECH, www.jtech.com/hospitality/hosp_index.htm, carries guest, manager and staff paging systems. Advanced Communications Equipment, www.advanced-ce.com, sells the Server Wireless Calling System for guests to signal servers. E-POS, www.eposonline.com/lrs.html, offers guest and server pagers to enhance communications and keep seats filled. Retail Wireless Communications, www.retail-wirelesscommunications.com/hospitality.htm, has systems that connect kitchen and servers.

Point-of-Sale Systems

- **POS systems.** POS systems can allow servers to concentrate on customer needs without running back and forth to the kitchen. They also shorten wait times at every stage of service. You'll reduce guest check errors because there's no more messy handwriting to decipher or math errors. You can monitor sales and productivity by food category, shift or table and enhance inventory-control systems. Plus, you can gather data to improve your scheduling procedures and adjust staffing levels based on accurate reports – even during mid-shift.

- **Purchasing a POS system.** Seek out "real world" experiences and recommendations. Ask vendors for local references and repair service contacts. Restaurant Report gives suggestions in their Q & A at www.restaurantreport.com/qa/possystem.html. The POS Help Desk, www.poshelpdesk.com, states, " We don't sell POS systems... We help you buy them!" Also, visit state, regional and national restaurant shows. You'll be able to demo and compare hardware, software and features at vendor booths. Finally, ask about report sharing and data exporting. To share statistics with your accountant, be certain that reports and/or raw data can exported or electronically linked with other systems.

Front-of-the-House Tools

Here are some practical ideas and helpful resources for labor-saving tools from the front door to the kitchen door.

- **Outfit workstations throughout larger dining rooms and exterior dining areas to reduce trips to the kitchen.** A self-contained workstation could include serving utensils and bowls, extra place settings and glassware; extra aprons and laundry bags; hot/cold beverage dispensers and coffeemakers; waste receptacles on wheels and mobile carts; undercounter dishwasher; salad and dessert assembly and service; POS systems, computer network and phone systems;

hand sink and/or utility sinks; ice machines and/or
storage units; and emergency clean-up supplies.

- **Incorporate self-service activities whenever
  possible.** Take care, as these may "turn off" customers
  or be negated by increasing food/beverage costs. Try
  placing menus in holders on each table. Create a
  beverage bar with hot and cold drink dispensers. See
  the Espresso Specialists Inc. at www.esi-
  online.com/Product/prod_frankesaphira.html) for the
  Saphira unit; perfect for self-service.

- **Install an automatic compacting trash receptacle.**
  Quick-service restaurants can reduce their trash
  containment labor by 1-2 hours a day with the Smart-
  Pack commercial trash receptacle in their stores.
  Manufactured by Waste Care, www.wastecare.com/
  Products-Services/Smart-Pack/main.htm, the Smart-
  Pack can also be programmed to "talk" to customers
  during use.

Back-of-the-House Equipment

Behind the swinging doors is your greatest opportunity for
incorporating labor-saving equipment and tools. There
are computerized ovens that can be programmed to bake and
hold entrées without anyone watching; conveyer belt
dishwashing systems that carry dishes from the serving area
to fully automated dishroom; and compact, multi-purpose
units that can be placed within easy reach.

- **Look for equipment that is easy to move, easy to
  clean and easy to operate.** Since looks aren't
  important in the kitchen, go for functionality over
  appearance.

- **Invest in quality materials so your staff doesn't
  waste time** tinkering, adjusting, operating, scrubbing
  or waiting for a repairperson.

- **Buy user-friendly.** Are the knobs placed within easy reach? Are labels, controls and instructions in plain view and easy to understand? Are emergency shut-offs well-marked? Check the buying guides and articles at FoodServicesSearch.com, www.foodservicesearch.com/Well_Equiped/index.cfm). This site requires free registration for full-access.

Purchasing Inventory Control and Kitchen Equipment

- **Consider computerizing your purchasing and inventory control.** Companies like Crunchtime, www.crunchtime.com, and Food Trak, www.foodtrak.com, offer software solutions. Many popular POS systems have inventory/purchasing capabilities or add-on modules.

- **Barcode systems** using hand-held printers and readers can streamline inventory management. Check out MRA Technologies at www.mra-tech.com to learn more. For Wine inventory-control systems in upscale establishments, see Wine Seller Pro, www.winesellerpro.com.

- **Web-based purchasing systems** can decrease your food and beverage purchasing costs according to Order Smart at www.ordersmart.com/ordersmart.

- **Coordinate and supervise your kitchen staff with a computer**. Intellikitchen®, a kitchen-management system, guides your staff through orders, recipe reminders and confirms what's in the to-go bag. You can find information at Apigent, www.apigent.com/solutions/intellikitchen/intellikitchen.html.

Prep Equipment

Saving even 30 minutes a day pays off! Here are some proven time savers:

- **Toss the Ginsu knife** and find a better way to peel, chop, dice, slice and shred.

- **Chop like a maniac with an electric vegetable processor.** Read what Foodservice Equipment Reports has to say at www.fermag.com/sr/v3i6_sr_fp.htm.

- **Peel a melon in 15 seconds** with the Univex PerfectPeeler, www.univexcorp.com. Peel and seeds are automatically separated from the melon. Quick-change blades adjust to accommodate everything from small cantaloupes to large honeydew.

- **Buy wedgers, cutters and slicers in a variety of sizes** with quick-replace blades and place them on a convenient workstation. Inconvenient, hard-to-use and out-of-sight equipment won't get used!

- **Produce up to 300 cookies per minute** with the Kook-E-King, www.kook-e-king.com, an automatic cookie depositer. The hopper can hold up to 90 pounds of dough, and more than 60 different dies are available.

- **Purchase combination prep machines for greater efficiency.** Is it a mixer that blends or a blender that mixes? Robot Coupe USA, www.robotcoupeusa.com/d1.html, produces a variety of food processors with multiple functions.

- **"Flatten and par-bake pizza crusts in seconds without skilled labor."** That's the claim of the PizzaPro by ProProcess Corporation, www.doughpro.com. Crusts can be prepared in less than 60 seconds and hold for hours for the lunch crowd. Crusts can also be frozen for later use.

- **Eliminate tears with an onion slicer.** Nemco Food Equipment, www.nemcofoodequip.com, specializes in food-prep equipment like the Easy Onion Slicer and the Green Onion Slicer Plus.

Cleaning Equipment

- **Dry dishes faster.** High-velocity air driers meet sanitation codes which means staff can be reusing or storing dishes faster.

- **Add a conveyer system to make it easier to move soiled dishware to the kitchen.** Adamation, Inc., www.adamationinc.com, manufacturers standalone conveyors and continuous-conveyor dishwashers.

- **Investigate the Power Soak System®** from Metcraft, Inc., www.metcraft.com/ps.html. This automated pot and pan wash sink manufacturer claims pot-washing labor savings of 65 percent and an 18-month payback.

Waste and Recycling Equipment

- **Place wet and dry waste receptacles and recycling bins near every work area.** These should be clearly marked and color coded for quick recognition. For faster handling, they must have casters or be placed on mobile carts.

- **Install indoor trash compactors.** Manufacturers state compactors can hold the equivalent of 15-20 trash bags (55-gallon) before emptying. To read other benefit information, log on to Waste Care's site at www.wastecare.com/Products-Services/Indoor-Compactors/Benefits.htm.

- **Set up a self-contained recycling system.** Waste Away Systems, wasteawaysystems.com, sells a compact, no-lift, no-touch reduction/recycling unit. Ver-Tech, www.ver-tech.com/select.html, manufacturers recycling equipment for baling cardboard, compacting plastic bottles and aluminum cans and handling other common restaurant waste products.

- **Switch to an outdoor trash compactor.** Helpful information on compactors can be found at Consolidated Equipment Corp., www.ceqp.com/ cptr_gen.htm, 323-583-5050. Manufacturers specializing in recycling and waste disposal management and equipment can be found at the Open Directory Project, www.dmoz.org, under the keywords "waste management" and "recycling."

Storage Fixtures

- **Use see-through storage containers** with spigots and drop-down doors or sliding lids for quicker access and inventorying and less handling.

- **Purchase refrigeration units capable of accommodating deliveries on pallets.** Walk-in cooler doors should be 4- to 5-feet wide for easy access.

- **Specify self-closing doors** or use a Thermal Flex Swing Door, www.walkinrefrigeration.com/ ThermalFlexSwingDoor.html.

- **Cut chilling times to speed handling steps.** Kolpak's, www.kolpak.com, Polar-Chill system blast chills products from above 140° F to 40° F in 2 hours.

- **Install a strip door to improve access and visibility** in storage rooms and walk-in coolers. Visit Strip Door World at www.stripdoorworld.com to learn more.

Cooking Equipment

- **Cook faster.** Microwave, conveyor, convection and impingement (pressured hot air) ovens are all energy- and labor-savers. Match your needs with the proper equipment. Some high-speed methods handle specific cooking and baking tasks better than others. Explore combination ovens that combine microwave technology with convection or impingement. These ovens provide the speed of microwaves without the taste and appearance negatives often associated with microwave cooking. Investigate lightwave/microwave countertop ovens from the Vulcan-Hart Company, www.vulcanhart.com. Speed claims of 50-75 percent, compact size (30" x 16"), and programming capabilities make the VIVA model worth considering.

- **Make your cook super-human.** Conveyor cooking technology and Blodgett's, www.blodgett.com, 36-inch Magigrill means one person can cook up to 250 burgers or 200 pieces of fresh chicken per hour.

- **Research air-door ovens.** Lang Manufacturing, 425-349-2400, builds "doorless" energy-efficient pizza ovens. Forced air keeps the heat in and gives operators quick access and easy product viewing.

- **Learn more about "speed" cooking** at Florida Energy Extension Service, www.agen.ufl.edu/~fees/pubs/ovens.html. An excellent source for information on energy-efficient commercial kitchen cooking equipment can be found at Gas Food Equipment Network, www.gfen.org/content/foodservice/equipment.html. Or see the Microwave Association, www.microwaveassociation.org.uk/factsheets/caterers.htm, for commercial microwave oven information Lincoln Products, www.lincolnfp.com has impingement oven information.

- **Cool and cook in one unit.** Minimal service and display kitchens frequently have space limitations. Even in large kitchens, combination equipment can save unnecessary steps, lifting and reaching.

- **Search for equipment that satisfies multiple functions** such as Imperial Commercial Cooking Equipment's Sizzle 'n Chill™ stovetop/refrigeration

unit, www.imperialrange.com. Investigate Rankin-
Delux's hot plate/wok combo, 800-345-4752 (West),
800-338-4325 (East). Look into Thermomix USA's 12-
in-1 appliance that whips, blends, chops, kneads,
steams and cooks, www.thermomix.com.

More Cooking-Equipment Tips

- **Free up employees with built-in temperature probes**
  and loud notification buzzers.

- **Increase productivity, food quality and safety with
  accurate thermometers.** Read Culinary.net's article at
  www.culinary.net/articlesfeatures/safeside/simplify-
  cooking.html.

- **Use portion-control dispensers for everything you
  can!** You'll not only trim food costs, but your staff will
  be working more efficiently.

- **Move the kitchen out front.** Display kitchens aren't
  just popular with customers. They are great fun for
  show-off chefs and free up space in the back. Food is
  cooked in full view and within steps of diners.

- **Reduce grease-handling activities.** Install a central
  grease collector. Contract with a company that delivers
  oil to remote tanks. Clean oil is piped directly to fryers
  and used fat is piped out for recycling. Or, purchase an
  "oil-free" fryer, where "frying" is done through infrared
  technology or flash heat activates the oil already in
  frozen, pre-browned foods.

- **Add a refrigerated base to the workstation.** Silver
  King, www.silverking.com/cb.shtml, makes models that
  hold six or ten full-size pans.

- **Use Sterno's Smart Can™ for buffet and chafing**

dishes. The built-in heat indicator tells workers at a glance that the can needs changing.

Beverage Tips

- **Select ice machines and bins that can be filled, emptied and cleaned easily.** Add long-handled food-safe scoops to help shorter workers access ice.

- **Invest in a gravity-fed ice system.** No more wasted labor lugging and loading ice with Follet's Ice Storage and Transport systems, www.follettice.com. Follet anticipates a typical restaurant can save up to one full-time worker per month every year!

Other Cooking Innovations

- **Don't wrap and rewrap pans.** Use see-through lids for steam-table pans from Cambro, www.cambro.com.

- **Tired of waiting for the pot to fill with water?** Wall-mounted flow fillers are available from Fisher at www.fisher-mfg.com, 800-421-6162.

- **Need a sharp edge fast?** Edgecraft's, www.edgecraft.com, Chef's Choice knife sharpener can hone a razor-sharp edge in 60 seconds and re-sharpened knives in less than 15 seconds.

- **Never scrap off a steam-table pan label again.** Buy wash-off labels from DayMark Food Safety Systems 800-847-010, www.dissolveaway.com.

- **Install an air door between hot and cold areas to preserve energy and improve traffic flow.** Visit Air Door World at www.airdoorworld.com for information.

Labor-Saving Equipment Resources

Food service equipment manufacturers are constantly introducing models designed to save you labor costs, floor space, energy costs and service costs. We've put together a brief list of commercial cooking equipment manufacturers to get you started you towards working smarter, not harder.

- **Ask your local food service equipment distributor about the brands most commonly** used in your community. Visit your local test kitchens at trade schools, utility companies and equipment resellers.

- **Select a model that suits your needs and budget.** Many manufacturers offer a broad range of equipment and models from which to choose.

EQUIPMENT NAME/MODEL MFG./SUPPLIER INFO	FUNCTION(S)
TurboChef TurboChef (www.turbochef.com)	Bake, roast, poach, air-fry
Convertible Buffet System SpringUSA (www.springusa.com)	Multi-purpose buffet setup with induction heating system
Combi-Steamers Rational (www.rationalusa.com)	Combination steamer, convection oven, broiler, braising pan, kettles, holding cabinet
Various Lang Manufacturing (www.langworld.com)	Computerized ovens, air-door pizza ovens, Clamshell (2-sided) griddles
Low-temp dishwashers Auto-Chlor Systems (check Yellow Pages)	Warewashing rental system
Cook & Hold Oven Alto Shaam (www.alto-shaam.com)	Radiant heat system for cooking ahead
CombiCraft CCG Series Cleveland Range (www.clevelandrange.com)	Hot air/convection heating, pure steam or combination convection/ steam for moister foods
Gas and Electric Combis with V-Air® System NU-VU (www.nu-vu.com)	Steam, dry bake, bake with steam, retherm, reconstitute, poach, roast, slow cook, proof, hold and warm
Various Restaurant Equipment World (www.restaurantequipment.net)	

Manufacturer Lists, Articles, Reviews and Other Resources

Food Service Central
www.foodservicecentral.com

Gas Foodservice Equipment Network
www.gfen.org/content/foodservice/equipment.html

Supply and Equipment Food Service Alliance
www.sefa.com

Food Service Equipment Reports
www.fermag.com

FoodService.com
www.foodservice.com

Food Service Equipment Magazine
www.fesmag.com

ESelNet Food Service (used equipment)
www.eselnet.com

Kitchen-Today (small equipment, tools)
kitchens-today.com

A Guide to Purchasing Food Service Equipment from the USDA
www.nal.usda.gov:8001/Training/equipment/equipment.html

CHAPTER NINE

FINANCIAL DECISIONS

As a restaurant owner, you're responsible for the tough decisions. This section provides you with decision-making support based upon financial considerations. Remember that numbers aren't the only way to determine the fate of your employees or your business. Time and time again, making the "wrong" financial decision has rewarded business owners with loyalty, dedication and unending support from customers, employees and the community. The key is to understand all the facts and your options and balance this all with the needs of your people.

Accounting Assistance

General and restaurant-specific accounting assistance can be found at:

- **Virtual Restaurant** (www.virtualrestaurant.com) offers "financial modeling for restaurant ventures" – business plans, spreadsheets.

- **General accounting terms** at integrainfo.com/ free/Glossary-V1-9.htm.

- **Restaurant-specific training for in-house bookkeepers** at Bookkeepers in the Restaurant Industry, www.bribri.com.

- **Local CPAs and accounting firms.** We recommend that you find a firm with extensive restaurant industry experience.

Cost Analysis Terms

Below are some analysis concepts and terms you may find helpful to make labor-saving decisions.

- **Prime cost.** Cost of food and beverage sold and the associated payroll.

- **Payroll costs.** Comprised of hourly pay rate, fringe benefits costs and employee productivity.

- **Productivity factor.** How much one employee can get done in one hour. Typically expressed as covers.

- **Covers.** Each individual diner is counted as one cover. Total covers are all diners during a set period (shift, hour). Covers can also be calculated on an average by dividing the total by a unit of time. 800 covers per shift = 100 average covers per hour.

- **Labor hours.** Total hours by all hourly production/service employees during a set period.

- **Fixed-cost employees.** Minimal staff needed without regard to sales volume.

- **Variable-cost employees.** Additional staff scheduled based upon sales volume.

What Are My Payroll Costs?

The chart on the following page has four employees with hourly rates from $5.15 to $8.10 per hour (including all payroll taxes) plus variable fringe benefits. For the purposes of this exercise, we've made assumptions about benefit costs and productivity measurements and left out payroll taxes as these costs affect the results.

At first glance, you'd think that Smith was your least-expensive employee (see Cost Ranking). But when you factor in each employee's productivity (see Covers Per Hour), you discover that Hernandez, the highest-paid employee with the greatest service capabilities, is your most cost-effective. Hernandez actually costs you 23.5-percent less per customer than Smith. You can see that you're better off financially to employ fewer, more productive employees and pay them more!

SERVER LABOR COSTS

EMPLOYEE	Hernandez	Lee	Benson	Smith
Hourly Pay	$8.10	$7.55	$6.00	$5.15
Hourly Fringe	$2.10	$2.00	$1.45	$1.00
Cost Ranking (Pay + Fringe)	4	3	2	1
Covers Per Hour	6	20	18	12
Cost Per Cover (Pay + Fringe ÷ Cust./Hour)	$0.39	$.048	$0.41	$.051
Productivity Ranking	1	3	2	4

Labor Cost Calculations

The following five ratios are used to compare labor costs and productivity against sales. Restaurant A and Restaurant B will be used throughout this section to illustrate formulas and the preferred results.

(Please note: Numbers used have no relationship to restaurant industry standards/averages. Rounding may slightly affect some results.)

	Restaurant A	Restaurant B
Sales	$34,500	$38,000
Profit *(sales less 40-percent food costs less payroll costs less $4692 other expenses)*	$5,175 (15%)	$6,238 (16.4%)
Payroll – administrative *(A has $25/hr. avg., B has $27.65/hr avg.)*	$2,760	$3,040
Payroll – hourly *(A has $14.73/hr. avg., B has $14.82/hr avg.)*	$8,073	$8,893
Covers	2,450	2,715
Sales Per Cover *(average)*	$14	$14
Labor Hours – administrative	110	110
Labor Hours – hourly	548	600

- **Traditional labor cost ratio.** Total payroll (salaried administrative and hourly) divided by total sales. The lower the percentage, the better. Many industry experts believe management salaries (fixed costs) should be listed separately as administrative expenses so as not to distort production and service (variable) labor calculations. Management costs would typically add 8-14 percent if included in payroll cost figures. This is the least-effective method of calculating true labor costs.Example below shows A and B have the same labor percentage with this method but this calculation does not reflect true productivity and profitability.

	Restaurant A	Restaurant B
Total Payroll ÷ Sales	$10,833 ÷ $34,500	$11,933 ÷ $38,000
Traditional Labor Cost Ratio	31.4% (8% fixed)	31.4% (8% fixed)
A and B have the same total labor cost percentages, although B pays more on average.		

- **Sales per labor hour.** Total sales divided by number of hours worked. The larger the dollar result, the better. Does not take into account that ticket averages are lower at breakfast than lunch and lunch lower than dinner. Best used for calculating variable labor. Not an accurate basis for scheduling, as it assumes consistent customer numbers throughout the period and check averages don't vary from breakfast to dinner.

	Restaurant A	**Restaurant B**
Sales ÷ Total Employee Hours	$34,500 ÷ 658	$38,000 ÷ 710
Sales Per Labor Hour	$52.43	$53.52
B sells $1.09 more per employee hour.		

- **Covers per labor hour.** Covers divided by non-administrative labor hours. The larger the result, the better. Best for historical comparisons and scheduling. Covers will vary based upon job category. Even fractional improvements can significantly improve your profitability. If either restaurant increased covers per labor hour by 1 person per hour, the annual sales increase would be $88,200. If Restaurant A servers increased their covers per hour to 22, the owner would need approximately 1 fewer servers per 18-hour day.

	Restaurant A	**Restaurant B**
All Production & Service Staff		
Covers ÷ Total Hourly Employee Hours	2,450 ÷ 658	2,715 ÷ 710
Covers Per Labor Hour	3.72	3.82
Servers Only		
Covers ÷ Total Server Hours	2,450 ÷ 136	2,715 ÷ 123
Covers Per Labor Hour	18	22
B has more productive employees.		

- **Labor costs per labor hour.** Total hourly payroll divided by number of hours worked. Best for historical comparisons. Must factor in cost of experienced employees versus less skilled workers and trainees.

	Restaurant A	**Restaurant B**
Hourly Payroll ÷ # Hourly Employee Hours	$8,073 ÷ 548	$8,893 ÷ 600
Labor Cost Per Labor Hour	$14.73	$14.82
A pays $0.09 less per employee hour.		

- **Labor cost per cover.** Total hourly payroll divided by the total covers (number of customers served). This calculation can be used for shift, day, weekly and monthly calculations. The lower the result, the more efficient the operation.

	Restaurant A	Restaurant B
Total Hourly Payroll ÷ Total Covers	$8,073 ÷ 2,450	$8,893 ÷ 2,715
Labor Cost Per Cover	$3.30	$3.28
B has a $0.02 lower labor cost per cover making it more productive than A.		

To Recap

Each labor cost calculation reveals more information about the productivity of Restaurants A and B.

- Both have the same total labor cost and 8 percent fixed labor percentage.
- B sells 2.1 percent more per employee hour.
- B is 2.7 percent more productive and can easily serve 40 people more per 8-hour shift.
- A pays 2.1 percent less per hour but its productivity is adversely affected.
- B has a less than 1 percent lower labor cost per cover than A.

Restaurant B is the overall winner – it's employees make more, they are more efficient and the restaurant has a larger profit!

Return on Investment

This example illustrates the potential return on investment (ROI) in purchasing labor-saving equipment. A ten-store restaurant chain is considering a new POS system. This chain posts annual sales of $10 million with a 40-percent food-cost factor. Their existing POS system is inadequate and is not linked to the corporate office. The chain will pay for the hardware and software in year one. We'll calculate hard cost savings (direct labor costs) and discuss soft cost savings for this new system. Corporate tax benefits of equipment purchases are not addressed in this exercise. Remember, these are hypothetical situations – real world results won't be this obvious.

EQUIPMENT OWNERSHIP

Purchase

Hardware (5 terminals per store @ $2,100 each)	$10,500
Software (including new modules)	$20,000
Total per store	$30,500
x 10 stores	$305,000

On-going Upkeep

Annual Maintenance Cost (15% of hardware cost)	$1,575
Software training, technical support (15% of software cost)	$3,000
Total per store	$4,575
x 10 stores	$45,750
First year costs for chain	**$350,750**
Annual amortized ownership costs (5-year life)	$70,150

HARD COST SAVINGS

Cost of an employee to call each store for nightly financial reports and produce recap report.

$40,000 salary x 1.25 (benefits) = $50,000 x 25%   **$12,500**

1/8 of the restaurant manager's time for labor scheduling and inventory per restaurant.

$50,000 x 10 (per store) x 1.25 (benefits) x 12.5%   **$78,125**

New labor module warns of approaching overtime – saving $10,000 per store annually.

$10,000 x 10   **$100,000**

New inventory module gives greater control to reduce shortage and waste.

Estimated savings is 1.5% of $4 million food costs   **$60,000**

Automated timekeeping for more accurate time reporting to prevent employees from arriving before shift and/or staying late.

Estimated savings is 10 hours weekly per store per year $26,000
(10 hours x 10 stores x 52 weeks = 5,200 hours x $5 overtime cost)

TOTAL FIRST YEAR HARD COST SAVINGS FOR CHAIN: $276,625

Soft Cost Savings

Soft costs savings are benefits that are not easily translated to numbers but have a beneficial impact on productivity and profitability. Your management experience and anecdotal information from POS vendors can help you with anticipatory savings. Some of the benefits include alleviating frustration with a slow, difficult-to-use system that may be contributing to absenteeism, lower job performance, lower morale and greater turnover. Quicker data entry times and increased customer service levels. Quicker training times and improved productivity. Expandable to handle future chain growth.

Simple ROI

ROI = Gain – amortized investment costs
ROI % = Gain – investment costs / investment costs

Our "gain" is the hard and soft cost savings.

Hard + Soft Cost Savings Per Year	$276,625 + $50,000 = $326,625
Investment	$70,150 per year
Return on Investment	$256,475 first year 366% ROI first year
Lifetime Savings (We'll assume no changes for this exercise)	$326,625 x 5 years = $1,633,125
Total Investment (Initial cost + 5 years of maintenance & training)	$305,000 + ($45,750 x 5) = $533,750
Return on Investment	**$1,099,375 total; 206% total**

Purchasing the POS system is a wise investment for this chain with an overall return of 206%. For more information on ROI and other financial-decision tools, see the Business Case Analysis site from Solution Matrix at www.solutionmatrix.com.

Man vs. Machine

Calculating the short- and long-term cost benefits of investing in labor-saving equipment can be difficult as there are many factors such as comparing purchasing to leasing, affects on cash flow, depreciable or deductible tax benefits and unpredictable repair costs. However, if you take away these variable and break it down into some basic numbers, you'll have enough information to make good purchasing decisions. This example looks at purchasing a commercial meat slicer that will save 30 minutes per day. This exercise will illustrate how even a relatively inexpensive piece of equipment saving only half an hour daily can put money in your pocket!

OWNERSHIP COSTS

Equipment Cost + (Annual Maintenance Costs x Lifespan) = Total Ownership Cost

$595 meat slicer with $25 upkeep x 5 years   **Total Ownership Cost: $720**

$595 + $125 (Divide by Lifespan of 5 years) **Annual Ownership Cost: $144**

ESTIMATED LABOR SAVINGS

Estimated Savings x Payroll Cost x # Days Used Annually = Yearly Labor Savings
(man-hours per day) (User's average hourly)

    .5   x $7.95 x 350   **Yearly Labor Savings = $1,391.25**
                                        Weekly Labor Savings = $26.75

RECOVERY

5-Year Ownership Cost	Divide by Weekly Savings	Paid for in the
$720	$26.75	27th week

In approximately 6 months, the labor savings paid for the slicer and the anticipated maintenance costs for the remaining 4 and a half years! You'll continue to save labor dollars.

Total net savings over the 5 years = $6,260.63!

Helpful Labor Facts and Resources

- Did you know that a typical fast-food establishment can serve 100 customers with 10.5 hours of labor while it takes over 70 hours for a full-service restaurant to handle the same number?

- Eight out of ten salaried restaurant workers started as hourly workers.

- More than 37 percent of all adult employees have worked in a restaurant at some time in their lives.

- The restaurant industry is the largest private-sector employer with 11.6 million workers.

- Salaries and wages in a median basis represented 30.3 percent of sales for full-service operations with average per-person checks of $15 or less. (National Restaurant Association's 2001 Restaurant Operations Report).

Productivity Resources

- Cost-Watch, www.cost-watch.com.

- Knowledge Storm, www.knowledgestorm.com.

- Food Cost Control Using Microsoft® Excel for Windows by Warren Sackler and Samuel R. Trapani, see www.atlantic-pub.com.

- National Restaurant Association, www.restaurant.org/research/op_ratios.cfm.

INDEX